CU00734263

Walking the Path
What it means to be a Buddhist

Michael Kewley
Dhammachariya Paññadipa

Copyright © Michael Kewley 2006
Second Edition 2007

ISBN 978-1-899417-05-6

Published by:
Panna Dipa Books.
E-mail:
dhammateacher@hotmail.com

Typeset & cover design by
Akaliko
E-mail:
akaliko@free.fr

Walking the Path

Dedication

I dedicate this book to the memory of my teacher
Sayadaw Rewata Dhamma,
who showed me how to live, and how not to live.

Walking the Path

Authors note

This book was originally written in 1982, under the title, 'The Western Lay Buddhist'. It is the first book I ever wrote. It was then handed to my teacher, Sayadaw Rewata Dhamma to read and approve. This he did, and since his approval was all I really wanted, my work was complete and the book was left in a box, untouched until February 2006.

Acting on the insistence of certain friends and disciples, this rediscovered book is now produced in its original form but with a new and more appropriate title. The words and style of writing are an illustration of my early years as a Buddhist disciple, and this I have not changed. Consequently, it is a book about the responsibility of calling oneself a Buddhist, although now I would not speak in this way.

The Buddha told us that in the end everything we carry must be put down and walked away from, even calling oneself a Buddhist. This I have done, and as always I offer my gratitude and deepest respect to all my teachers, but in particular the late Sayadaw Rewata Dhamma.

The true spiritual path is beyond names, style and labels. We are required to open our heart and live a life of love and awareness.

For me as a former disciple of a master, the true path was always to hear, test and then apply the wisdom of the Buddha.

In my teachings now twenty five years later, the words are different, but the Path is the same.

May all beings be well and happy.

Walking the Path

Stories from the Dhammapada

The Dhammapada is part of the Khuddaka Nikaya (shorter discourses) section of the Suttanta Pitaka of the Theravada tradition of Buddhism.

These short verses were given by the Buddha on various occasions during his forty five year ministry, to emphasise and explain different aspects of his teaching and the Dhamma.

In its complete form each verse is accompanied by the short story that gave occasion for the verse to be uttered.

I have used the inspirational verses from the Dhammapada liberally throughout the book, but for the section of the Ten Wholesome Actions I have also used the stories to present the verses as a way to illustrate the different teachings.

All references have been taken from the 'Dhammapada - verses and stories', produced by the Burma Pitika Association.

Walking the Path

Introduction

By modern standards Buddhism can rightly claim to be an ancient religion. It was established upon the enlightenment and subsequent teachings of Siddhartha Gotama, the former prince of a small kingdom nestling in the foothills of the Himalayas near the border of what is now Nepal, almost two thousand six hundred years ago.

Shocked by the realities of human existence, Siddhartha renounced his princely life and all the luxuries that it contained and became a wandering ascetic, determined to find the answers to the questions that had driven him from the royal palace.

He wanted to know the purpose of life. What is the reason for human birth when it inevitably leads to inescapable misfortune such as old age, sickness and finally death? What was the point of it all when suffering, both gross and subtle, seem to pursue mankind endlessly?

Overcome by the need to understand the reason for taking birth he renounced his earlier splendour and embarked upon a spiritual quest. This quest lasted six years until finally, after many trials and tribulations, he arrived at perfect understanding. Enlightenment. It was the full moon day of May in the forest of Uruvela, now the holy town of Budh Gaya in Northern India. Sitting in meditation under a giant Peepul tree he gained complete knowledge of the nature of man. Of why we are born and of why suffering and unhappiness are so tightly interwoven into our existence.

With this understanding he earned himself the title 'Buddha' meaning the Awakened One, the one who is no longer asleep to the true nature of the universe.

For forty five years after his enlightenment he wandered throughout Northern India teaching any and all who would ask for guidance, and gathering around him beings who, because of his great compassion and perfect instruction, would become enlightened themselves, and so continue the tradition that has become known to the world as Buddhism, the teachings of an enlightened being.

Since the time of Siddhartha these teachings have spread throughout the world and have been accepted by many cultures, but it is only within the past sixty years that it has made an impact in the west. Many people now in Europe and America are interested in Buddhism and Buddhist teachings, having read books, seen television documentaries and possibly even spoken to the growing number of resident monks and nuns, but feel at a loss when attempting to transfer these teachings from their background of Eastern culture, into their ordinary, everyday Western lives.

Many people in the West, it seems, would like to consider themselves Buddhist, basing their understanding on what they have read or heard, but perhaps have never really had the opportunity to reflect upon the statement, 'I am a Buddhist,' and are therefore unaware of the extent of their own personal obligations towards this beautiful way of life and living.

If we take this statement seriously in our lives we must look at it not only from the context of our own spiritual development, but also from the wider position of our social and moral obligations, and against a background of correct religious understanding.

Buddhism is classified as one of the five major religions in the world alongside Judaism, Islam, Christianity and Hinduism and can claim more than four hundred million adherents worldwide. However, although there are many similarities with regard to fundamental moral practices between Buddhism and the other four religious paths, there is a chasm of difference when we consider the ultimate goal of practice, and even the method of practice itself.

For all theistic religions there is at the very core the concept of a creator god. A being who not only created the universe and all it contains, but also has the power and inclination to reward and punish us for our deeds. Accompanying this belief in a supreme being is the concept of the true self, soul or atman, a part of our human make up that is indestructible. It is a part of god himself. However, this true self, soul or atman, cannot be contacted by us in any way. It cannot be seen, touched or experienced in this lifetime and yet, is the divine connection between ourselves and god. The purpose of life therefore is to create the right conditions that will afford at death union with that being. It may take a single lifetime as in Judaism, Islam and Christianity, or countless rounds of existence as with Hinduism and other Eastern religions. The main and guiding factor of theistic religion is faith. Acceptance of what tradition has dictated as being true, and the belief that if its tenets are upheld salvation can be attained.

All theistic religions include acts of prayer and devotion where the supreme being, and often his messengers and prophets, are worshiped, and in some extreme forms still, animal sacrifice is demanded. In the name of this great being wars have been fought, atrocities committed and injustices performed, all with his apparent blessing. But this is his will, as interpreted by man.

As Buddhism teaches that no first cause can be found, that no being rewards or punishes our actions and that blind faith and belief should be completely disregarded in favour of extensive investigation into the reality of our existence, can it truly be called a religion at all?

The ultimate goal of Buddhist practice is not union with a supreme being, but the attainment of Nibbana. The complete release from any form of existence at all, for all rebirth, whether into a heaven realm, a hell realm or even the human realm, carries with it the suffering that is inherent in taking birth again.

Nibbana is not extinction, but a transcendent state that cannot be described in words. We can only point to what it is by saying what it is not. However, Nibbana is real, and more than that, realisable in this very lifetime. We don't have to wait until we are dead to experience it. It can be attained right here, right now!

To devoted Buddhists throughout the world the notion that belief and blind faith are prerequisites for acceptance onto the Buddhist path is a nonsense. As Buddhists we are invited to investigate and to explore the teachings given until we finally understand for ourselves, by our own direct experience. From this place we will know the validity of applying these teachings to our everyday life.

The teachings of Siddhartha Gotama, collected and collectively called 'Buddhism', can best be described, not as a religion, but more accurately, a Path of Wisdom. A way of life and living.

Michael Kewley
Dhammachariya Paññadipa
France
May 2006

Contents

Walking the Path

Walking the Path

Part One

Walking the Path

Background to Buddhist Understanding

The Buddha was born a human being, and attributed all his attainments to human endeavour. He made no divine claims at all and insisted that what was possible for him is possible for anyone who turns their attention towards the spiritual life under his guidance.

The goal of Buddhist practice is Nibbana, a transcendent state of being beyond human conceptualisation and free from any taints of greed, hatred and delusion, the three fires that burn within us all. Nibbana is realisable in this very lifetime. We don't have to die to know if it is real. The path to this goal is clearly marked by the Buddha based as it is upon is own experience, and is as applicable today as it was two thousand six hundred years ago in ancient India. This path requires clear comprehension into the human condition and explains that only through direct and personal experience, can we know the Truth.

By diligent practice, each one of us can come to understand completely the underlying reality of our existence and the truth of the universe as it unfolds, moment after moment.

In Buddhism there is no concept of a creator god or of an everlasting soul to reunite with him. There is no supreme being to reward or punish our good and bad actions, and no prayers or favour asking. Only the knowledge, developed through practice, that whatever we think, say or do, will have an effect on ourselves and the world around us. It is only the consequential effects of those thoughts, words or actions that will wait for us in the future. No reward, no punishment, only consequence. This, simply put is the Buddhist teaching of Kamma - the law of cause and effect.

If we turn to the Dhammapada, part of the Suttanta Pitika and probably the most popular of all the Buddhist scriptures, we find the teaching of Kamma contained within the first two verses:

We are what we think.
All that we are arises with our mind,
and with our mind we create our world.
Speak or act with an impure mind
and difficulties will follow you,
as the wheel follows the ox
that pulls the cart.

We are what we think.
All that we are arises with our mind,
and with our mind we create our world.
Speak or act with a pure mind
and happiness will follow you
like your shadow in the brightest part of the day,
inseparable.

Dhammapada: verses 1&2

Buddhism has been called, 'the religion of science' because of its investigative nature. No blind faith here, no mere acceptance of dogma and doctrine, only the continued probing of Truth until all questions fall away and complete liberation, Nibbana is attained.

The Buddha always advised an open minded attitude to spiritual study as opposed to the cultivation of belief, and expresses it quite forcefully in a discourse to the Kalamas:

At one time the Buddha visited the small town of Kesaputta in the kingdom of Kosala. The people of this town were known by the common name of Kalama, and were not strangers to visiting holy men.

When they heard that the Buddha had arrived they went eagerly to see him and hear him expound his teachings like so many of the others had done in the past. However the Buddha remained silent until someone asked a question.

"Sir, there are many wandering teachers passing through our town, each one criticising the others, and all expounding their own doctrine, and in doing so paint an important picture of themselves and their teaching, whilst at the same time depreciating the teachings of others. Such, however, is the strength of their argument that it is difficult for us to know who is telling the truth and who we should follow."

"People of Kalama," replied the Buddha, "You are wise to doubt and question the teaching of such men, for acceptance of teachings without wisdom leads only to suffering. Therefore Kalamas do I say to you; do not go upon what has been acquired by repeated hearing, nor upon tradition, nor upon rumour, nor upon scripture, nor upon surmise, nor upon axiom, nor upon the consideration 'this monk is our teacher', but only Kalamas when you know for yourselves, 'these things are good, these things are without blame, these things are praised, undertaken and observed by the wise and lead to the benefit and happiness of all', should you enter and abide in them."

Excerpt from the Kalama Sutta

The Buddha wanted us to make the best possible use of this wonderful opportunity as a human being, to work toward and attain complete liberation from all the pain, suffering and despair that this life can bring. However, we can only do that through self realisation, total understanding of the Truth, and not through becoming lost in a system of belief and blind faith.

Often when asked about his teaching he would reply, 'Ehi passiko', 'Come and see, experience it for yourself'.

When questioned by the Brahmins, the guardians of the religious knowledge, if he taught of a god or a soul, he would not answer, but maintain a Noble Silence, indicating that the question by its very nature, was already based on an assumption. To give any answer, therefore would only be misleading, and a misunderstanding concerning his teaching would arise. Rather, he would recommend that they listen to his words and apply them to their own lives. In that way they would be able to discern the Truth for themselves and then be in a position to teach others.

It is clear then that Buddhism is not a religion of blind faith and worship, but rather a way of life established in reason and direct experience of the Truth. The Buddha, whose intellectual mind must have been at least as bright as the best of the great thinkers and philosophers of the day, did not encourage idle speculation about life and the universe.

In one well known story the Buddha actually admonished a monk for attempting to blackmail him into making speculative statements.

Malunkyaputta was a monk training with the Buddha. He had received instruction and been given his object for meditation, but he found that he could not concentrate because of the restless nature of his mind. His head was filled with the big questions of life that he felt he must have the answers to. Questions such as, 'Is the universe finite or infinite? Is it eternal? What is the nature of god and the essence of the soul?'

Eventually he could bear it no longer and craved an audience with the Buddha. Once received, he put forward his questions and the real reason for his visit.

"Sir," he began, "I have been following you in the holy life for some time now and I have repeatedly asked you for answers to my questions. However, each time I ask, you fob me off with an unsatisfactory explanation. I have reached the position now whereby if you will not give me a satisfactory answer I will leave this order of monks and go elsewhere. After all, if you know, why not say? And if you don't know, why not just come straight out and say 'I don't know Malunkyaputta,' for there can be no shame in that."

"Malunkyaputta," answered the Buddha, "Did I ever say to you 'Come Malunkyaputta, follow me in the holy life and I will explain such things to you?' No Malunkyaputta I did not, and why? Because these things have no value to those seeking the Truth.

Malunkyaputta, I have explained all that needs to be known for those attempting to live the holy life, and whatever opinions you may form with regard to your questions, they will not help you in your everyday life. Therefore Malunkyaputta, accept what I have taught about old age, sickness and death, suffering, its cause, its cessation and the way that leads to that cessation, and do not concern yourself with the things that I have not spoken of."

The Buddha then continued with a story.

A man was found lying on the ground, his leg pierced by a poisoned arrow. Quickly his friends and relatives rushed to his side to carry him off to the nearest doctor. However, the wounded man would not allow himself to be moved until he had certain things explained to him. He wanted to know the name of the man who had shot him, to which caste he belonged, whether his skin was light or dark and if he was tall and thin or short and stout or of medium build. He also wanted to know which type of wood the bow was made from and with which poison the arrow was tipped.

And so it went on. So many questions to be answered before the actual work of healing could take place. In such a situation there is simply not the need to know such things, and so the wise person concerns themselves with what is important and ignores that which has little or no value.

Buddhism then, is a path of doing, not of discussion and speculation. It is a method of self realisation leading to the highest goal of liberation, Nibbana.

To say, 'I am a Buddhist,' means that we are actively engaged in understanding our own reality through contemplating and reflecting upon the teachings of the Buddha.

It will also mean that we are seriously involved in a daily meditation practice and making sincere efforts to live our life in a right and beautiful way.

With such an understanding the benefits of practice are bound to come to us, and not only us, but ultimately all beings will benefit from our selfless efforts.

The Four Noble Truths
&
The Journey to Enlightenment

Walking the Path

The First Noble Truth
Suffering

'Only one thing do I teach,
suffering and the release from suffering.'

The Four Noble Truths are the heart and foundation of the teaching of the Buddha. They are the very essence of Buddhism, for within them is contained the problem, the cause of the problem, the solution to the problem and the means to arrive at that solution.

All the many and varied schools and traditions of Buddhism have as their central theme, the Four Noble Truths and in fact, the whole of the Buddhas subsequent teaching is nothing more than the further analysis and investigations into these truths. It was only the complete and intuitive understanding of the Four Noble Truths that transformed Siddhartha from a struggling worldling into a Buddha.

As Buddhists, lay or monastic, our whole practice is directed towards understanding the significance of this great teaching. In brief the Noble Truths are:

The truth of suffering.
The truth of the cause of suffering.
The truth of the cessation of suffering.
The path that leads to the cessation of suffering.

The First Noble Truth concerns suffering.

Suffering is the over simplistic translation of the Pali word, Dukkha, which is used to describe the human condition. For convenience I will use the word suffering after I have given a few words of explanation.

Dukkha has no direct equivalent in the English language because its range of meaning is so subtle and so vast. It is the word used by Buddhists to describe the inherent unsatisfactoryness of human existence and extends from the most severe physical pain and mental anguish, to the slightest itch that must be scratched, or the vaguest feeling of doubt, worry or uncertainty. From the moment we are born we experience Dukkha.

We are too hot or too cold, too hungry or too full, too tired or too restless. Our family, friends, colleagues and even lovers continually fail to please and satisfy us, and we find ourselves always struggling to achieve that point of balance we call happiness. However, even happiness is Dukkha. Not because it is painful or unpleasant, far from it, happiness is what we seek to escape the painful and the unpleasant, but because it cannot, and does not endure. Happiness is happiness, but happiness is Dukkha. We cannot manufacture it at will, or create the perfect conditions for its arising with any certainty. Even to repeat once successful formulas cannot guarantee the appearance of happiness. Happiness comes and goes by itself and so is unsatisfactory. This is why happiness is Dukkha.

This, in brief, is the quality of Dukkha, and the realisation of this was the first part of the Buddhas enlightenment.

Seven weeks after his enlightenment at the foot of the Bodhi tree in what is now Budh Gaya, the Buddha set out for the deer sanctuary at Sarnath, just outside Varanasi. Here he met again his five former disciples who had deserted him just before his enlightenment.

In his first teaching as an enlightened being, he outlined to these five former disciples, the Noble Truth of Dukkha, suffering.

> This, bhikkhus, is the Noble Truth of Suffering:
> Birth is suffering, decay is suffering,
> disease is suffering, death is suffering.
> Association with unloved ones is suffering,
> separation from loved ones is suffering.
> Not to get what one wants is suffering.
> In short, the five aggregates* of grasping are suffering.

Dhammacakkapattavana Sutta

Perhaps our first reaction to hearing this First Noble Truth is one of despair. Everything it seems, is suffering. Nothing is excluded. Life itself could be seen as a futile endeavour, always struggling towards happiness and yet always being thwarted by its impermanent and fleeting nature.
However, we must remember that Siddhartha was not yet the Buddha when he first began to investigate Dukkha, and it was in fact, only the continued examination of it that led to his enlightenment.

As a young prince, Siddhartha was raised into a life of luxury and ease. Wearing only the finest clothes, eating the most delicious food and passing his days in the company of family, friends and entertainers. A life that perhaps many of us would envy today. However, even in these perfect surroundings

---

The five aggregates here refer to the five aspects of our human nature that appear at birth. They are; body, feelings, perception, mental formations and consciousness.

he would often experience unhappiness, manifesting in its various forms as boredom, frustration, irritation and doubt. He realised that old age pursued him and all he loved accompanied by sickness and finally death. No-one could escape the relentless consequence of life, for death came to all, rich and poor, prince and pauper alike. What was the purpose of life, when rank and privilege, in the final analysis, meant nothing at all?

Against this background of doubt and spiritual turmoil he eventually arrived at a difficult decision. He would leave the palace and its worldly splendour and wander the land to find a purpose and reason for life. If he was successful and could discover why are beings born only to suffer, he would return to the palace and share his knowledge with his family and friends, so that they may enjoy real and lasting happiness.

On the night of the full moon of July in his twenty ninth year, Siddhartha Gotama prince to the Sakyan kingdom, silently stole out of the palace to begin his quest. He rode into the night until he was far enough from his home, cut off his long, black, flowing hair, removed his fine garments and replacing them with the simple robes of the holy man, began his life as a wandering ascetic.

In those days, as with now, the primary task of anyone embarking on a spiritual journey was to place themselves under a teacher of good reputation. This Siddhartha did.

He became the disciple of a famous teacher, Alarma the Kalama, a man who had discovered a very refined and subtle system of meditation, culminating in the experience of a state of mind known as 'The experience of nothingness.'

For many months Siddhartha worked diligently under his

teacher, quickly acquiring the meditation skills necessary to realise the goal of his practice, until one day Alarma the Kalama, announced that he could teach him no more. He had attained mastery!

Far from being pleased by this news, Siddhartha was despondent. He knew that this was not the final answer to the question of life and its suffering. Sadly, and with a heavy heart, he said goodbye to his teacher.

He now travelled to study with another famous teacher of the time, a man called Udaka Ramaputta. His system of meditation culminated in the state of mind known as 'Neither perception nor non perception.'

Once again Siddhartha practised earnestly and with a vigour unequalled by any other student, until one day he was informed that his journey was over. He had attained the highest state of meditation and was now as knowledgeable as his teacher. Udaka offered him the position as joint leader of the group and together they would teach all they knew.

However, once again Siddhartha was despondent. With the help and guidance of two of the most famous and reputable teachers of the time he had experienced mental states far beyond the everyday encounter, and yet no matter how subtle and refined these mental states were, he knew they did not hold the answer to the problems concerning the human condition. Old age, sickness and death. There was, it is true, a temporary suspension of suffering whilst experiencing the fruits of this practice, but at some point he had to rejoin the ordinary world to eat, sleep, bathe and perform the other usual human functions.

These meditations were a temporary escape from suffering,

but not the solution to it.

With sadness again he said goodbye to his teacher. It was now time for a new direction. Accompanied by five colleagues, disciples of Udaka who had been impressed by the determined efforts of Siddhartha, he set out for the forest area known as Uruvela, on the banks of the river Neranjara. Here they would live as a small community and practice asceticism, the other form of spirituality popular at that time.

The fundamental practice of the ascetic is the weakening of the body by special religious or spiritual practices in order to release the soul or spirit from its prison.

This Siddhartha, now known as the Ascetic Gotama, did all the while encouraged by the respect shown to him by his five companions who had now established him as their leader.

First Gotama stopped begging for food and began to live rough on wild berries and fruit. Even that was not enough for him. He reduced his food intake even further until it was minimal, just the tiniest amount necessary to support life. His body became thin and weak with his eyes resembling two stones inside a deep well. His hair fell out, and such was his state of emaciation, as he would later recount, that he only had to press his stomach to touch his spine. However, his contempt for the body did not end there. Other practices included holding his breath until the point of unconsciousness, sitting outside without shade in the hottest part of the day and sitting alone at night amongst the dead and decomposing corpses in the charnel grounds. This last act must certainly have tested his resolve, for fear of ghosts and hungry wild animals could not have been far from his mind.

These and other formidable practices became his daily routine, all the while watched by his five companions. According to the Buddhist commentaries Gotama became the greatest ascetic the world has ever seen, such was his dedication to the practice of mortification of the body.

Eventually the years of this strenuous mental and physical abuse came to perhaps the only possible conclusion. With mind and body at their lowest ebb, he collapsed from sheer exhaustion. He had still not found the answers to the questions of life. This then, was also not the road to the spiritual liberation he had been seeking.

At this point we may reflect upon the mental state of Gotama.

He had lived for twenty nine years as a royal prince, surrounded by the very best in splendour and comfort. He had a beautiful and loving wife Yashodhara, as well as parents and many friends who cared for him and his welfare. To many this must have seemed like the perfect life, and yet he had abandoned it. He had left the very people who loved and cared for him most and gone into the greater world alone. He had walked away from his one day old son, Rahula, and entered a way of life and living that was completely alien to him, that of the homeless wandering ascetic. He had trained with two of the foremost meditation teachers of the time and succeeded even their expectations. But, still dissatisfied with that, he had entered the ascetic path, the path of self mortification. For almost six years he had practiced earnestly in this way, and taken this path to its furthest extreme, but was still no nearer the goal he sought. The only result of this long endeavour was complete mental and physical exhaustion and total collapse. His despair must have been immense. His noble quest to find the answers to the deepest questions of life had ended in failure.

Perhaps thoughts like these ran through the mind of Gotama

as he lay in the dirt, his skeleton body too weak to support him and seemingly all hope gone. What more could he do? He had tried the known and accepted methods of liberation and they had all failed. What was left for him now?

It was at this point that he was discovered by a kindly shepherd who, recognising his immediate need, offered him some food and over the next weeks and months, nursed him back to his former robust self. However, on the first occasion of taking food, a bowl of milk rice, he was seen by his five companions who, out of disgust and contempt for his apparent lack of will and sincere determination, decided to leave him and strike out on their own. They walked away from him and continued their ascetic path at a deer park just outside Varanasi, called Isipatana. Gotama was now alone. As his strength returned he again and again contemplated what had gone before. As a prince, even with everything he could possibly desire, he had never been perfectly happy. There was always one more thing that could improve the situation. Also, always in his mind, would be the fallibility of the human condition. Old age, sickness and death. Out of desperation he had left that life behind and embarked upon a life of severe austerity. That life, even allowing for the knowledge gained through study with Alarma the Kalama and Udaka Ramaputta had served only to weaken him and place him at deaths door. It was now time for a different path.

As his health and vitality returned he remembered an incident from his youth, once long forgotten but now fresh in his memory.
It was the time of the ploughing festival, an annual fertility rite for the people of the Sakyan kingdom, and Siddhartha, as a small boy was taken to see the splendour of the occasion.

His father, the king would first parade in a cart drawn by two bullocks decked in golden trappings, whilst in order of social descent, nobles, artisans and farmers would follow, each in their finery. The festival lasted a long time with much socialising and laughter, but quickly as a little boy of seven years, Siddhartha grew bored with the spectacle and returned to the place where a special couch had been set up for him in the shade of a rose apple tree. Sitting quietly and alone he spontaneously entered into a state of meditation that at once left him calm and serene, yet with a heightened sense of awareness. He sat for some time in this way until he was discovered by his attendants. This was his first spiritual experience and the now fresh memory of it gave him a new direction for the future.

He began to practice and perfect this newly rediscovered form of meditation, at the same time continuing to build his body to its former level of good health until, so the tradition says, the thirty two marks of the future Buddha appeared on him.

On the day of his thirty fifth birthday the ascetic Gotama went to continue his now well established method of meditation at the foot of a tree close to the Neranjara river.

At that time, the lady Sujata, daughter of the local village headman, came to make an offering to the guardian deity who lived in that very tree. She had prepared a special pudding of rice and concentrated milk taken from the cream of thirty two cows and placed it in a golden bowl. However, on approaching the tree she saw Gotama, clean, handsome and radiant, sitting in perfect stillness and peace. A great joy arose in her as this vision met her eyes, and not knowing if she was encountering a man or a god, she made her offering to Gotama, paid her respects and returned home.

Gotama accepted the offering and proceeded to the river to

bathe and eat his meal. According to the Theravadin scriptures now something wonderful happened. When Gotama had finished his meal he placed the golden bowl on the water and said, 'If I am to attain enlightenment this day, may this golden bowl float upstream.'

As he released his hands from the bowl it gently began to move against the current until, in the middle of the river it was caught in a small whirlpool and pulled to the bottom, thus signifying the events that were to take place that would not only transform his life, but the lives of millions of beings worldwide.

For the rest of the day he relaxed and spent time in quiet contemplation preparing himself for the task ahead. Already in his mind was the vow that would establish him for all time as perhaps the greatest human being that has ever lived. This special and unique vow was that once his meditation had begun that evening, he would not move from that place until he was completely enlightened and worthy of the title Buddha.

As the sun began to set he crossed the river where he met the brahmin Sottiya, who presented him with a small gift of kusa grass to use as a cushion for his meditation.

As he walked through the forest he found a large tree perfect for his needs. He arranged the kusa grass at its base, positioned himself in the cross legged posture of meditation, faced the east, allowed his eyes to close and began the final part of his journey.

The Buddhist scriptures have full accounts of the events as they occurred, but suffice to say that after many hours of patient endurance, struggling with many desires and fantasies, dreams and memories, his mind began to clear understanding arose and the enlightenment took place.

For many years he had contemplated Dukkha , the suffering and general unsatisfactoryness inherent in all human existence and the struggles that all beings must endure by simply taking birth.

But now as the full moon of May was setting and the sun of a new day rising, he knew fully and completely the exact nature of man and Dukkha, and the inseparable relationship of the two.

The Second Noble Truth
The arising of suffering

With the realisation of the truth of suffering came also the knowledge of its cause. Unhappiness, unsatisfactoryness, pain, sorrow, suffering and all the other subtle and gross manifestations of Dukkha do not simply occur haphazardly, arising out of thin air to fall upon any innocent bystander. Rather, we are the manufacturers and architects of all our suffering, however otherwise it may seem.

This, bhikkhus is the Noble Truth
of the Cause of Suffering:
It is desire which leads back to birth,
along with the lure and the lust that finds pleasure
first here, then there, namely
the desire for sensual pleasure, the desire to be born again
and the desire for annihilation.

Dhammacakkappavattana Sutta

By making pleasant feelings in general and happiness in particular our main objectives in life we, in fact, ensure the continuation of our own personal Dukkha.
In the world of our senses we continually seek bigger, better and more fulfilling experiences. With our eyes we seek beautiful objects to gaze upon and with our ears we seek pleasant sounds to listen to. We favour only the most exquisite aromas to smell and the time and energy spent catering to our taste buds is almost beyond comprehension. Physical comfort is another way through which we expend enormous amounts of time and effort, and the all consuming desire to only experience the most pleasant mental states at the expense of

their opposites, completes the jigsaw picture of the sensual world. A picture that we can never hope to perfect.

By always choosing the pleasant experience over the unpleasant one, we reinforce the habit of placing ourselves at the centre of our own personal universe where, not only must everything revolve around us, it must also always please and satisfy us. With only a little reflection it is easy to see the truth of this as even in our own lives we always seek the bigger, the better and ultimately, the most satisfying experience. The result of this constant quest for perfection through the senses is Dukkha, the inevitable experience of unsatisfactoryness, as everything we put our hopes into to please us forever, eventually fails and leaves us once again seeking a new and stimulating replacement.

It is not possible for any of us to arrange the world to always be just the way we want it, and yet so much of our time is spent in exactly this activity, insisting that everything experienced through the five physical senses and even the mind itself be perfect for us, and never disappoint. Our friends, family, colleagues, lovers and even teachers, continually fail to live up to our expectation of them, and so we suffer. Our material possessions break, get lost or simply no longer interest us, and we suffer. It is inevitable.

In the wider view of social interaction, the same conditions apply. Politicians and government ministers fight and argue that opposing policies are wrong and doomed to failure, simply because they are not their policies. We believe all our plans and ideas are the best, if only because they are ours. We all believe that given the opportunity we could all put the world to rights, if only everyone would listen to us. Our views are the best views, it's as simple as that.

To live, tied as we are to the realm of sensual experience brings only unhappiness. Perhaps not immediately, but it is always inevitable.

Whatever we do to promote personal happiness by its very nature creates exactly the right conditions for its opposite.

The Buddha also spoke of two other forms of desire or attachment that when pursued, lead only to further suffering. These desires are as prominent today as they were in the time of the Buddha and still form the basis for religious argument. They are, the desire to be born again, to continue in some form beyond the human experience, whether in a heaven realm, close to god and his angels, or as a reincarnation, perhaps returning to earth as an animal, a human or even, as in the Tibetan tradition, a Rimpoche, a reincarnated high lama, and the desire for total annihilation, the complete end of everything, a perpetual dreamless sleep.

As we have already seen, the Buddha did not encourage speculation about the great mysteries of life. Rather, he taught a way whereby each one of us by our own efforts and without the assistance and involvement of guardian or ruling deities, can experience directly, the ultimate truth, and so know the most subtle aspects of human existence. Naturally, blind faith and belief play no part in this journey to liberation, and any clinging or attachment even to long held views or ideas should be abandoned immediately.

The belief that there is a soul or self, that is an integral part of each person, does not bring spiritual realisation. Nor does the belief that all existence is tied to the body and that at death there is no more.

Belief is not the truth, belief is what we cultivate when we don't know the truth!

The Second Noble Truth reveals that desire, craving and attachment, unheeded by the mind, are the origins of our unhappiness and unsatisfactory experiences with life, no matter if at times it seems otherwise.

Life is a bitter, though sugar coated sweet. We crave and desire things to make us happy only to find them inevitably inferior to the expectation.

The cycle of desire and expectation resulting in disappointment and unhappiness is endless.

Truly, we are born to suffer.

The Third Noble Truth
The cessation of suffering

At one time the Buddha was asked to explain his teaching to a group of Brahmins, to which he answered:

Only one thing do I teach,
suffering and the end of suffering.

So far we have only examined the suffering aspect which is inherent in our human condition. It is apparently inescapable and brought about entirely by ourselves. What then is the teaching that the Buddha claimed to have realised that will take us out of the reach of sorrow, suffering and the whole range of Dukkha?

It is here that the Third Noble Truth, shining as brilliantly as a beacon in the night, shows how we can release ourselves from our terrible on-going ordeal, by demonstrating that there is a way to bring about the end of suffering.

This Bhikkhus
is the Noble Truth of the cessation of suffering.
Truly it is the forsaking,
the release and the detachment
from these very desires.

Dhammacakkappavattana Sutta

This Third Noble Truth sounds so simplistic that it hardly deserves the title 'Noble', however, the path to spiritual awakening is not an easy path, but this truth is the key to walking it.

By eliminating the cause of suffering we naturally eliminate the experience of it. What could be simpler than that?

Once we let go of the desire to continually experience happiness and never unhappiness, of wanting to be warm, secure and well fed, to impress others and demanding only the best for ourselves, our family and friends, we let go of our experiences of suffering.

Once we learn to accept and 'simply be' with the world, even when we don't like or approve of the situations we find ourselves in, we will place ourselves in the position of spiritual balance. By no longer demanding that others always please and satisfy us, but allowing them to be who

and what they are, fully accepting and open to their faults and perceived shortcomings, we find peace with the world.

But how can we give up these desires and impulses that come to us as naturally as breathing?

How can we stop wanting things from a purely selfish and personal basis and develop the more open and beautiful qualities that have their foundations in love, compassion, joy and balance of mind?

To say that there is a way to the end of suffering is not enough. That way has to be revealed and demonstrated.

This is exactly what the Buddha did when he disclosed the Fourth Noble Truth.

The Fourth Noble Truth
The path that leads to the cessation of suffering.

The Buddha tells us that we should not suppress our desires, cravings and attachments, to continually push them away and not acknowledge them, nor does he tell us to simply indulge them, blindly following wherever they lead. Rather he teaches a middle way, a transcendent way whereby we can know fully all our desires and mental impulses, recognising that which is wholesome and that which is not, and act accordingly. This way, that teaches awareness and gentle restraint, leads to full spiritual understanding and is known as the Eightfold Path. This path is contained within the Fourth Noble Truth.

This, bhikkhus
is the Noble Truth of the Path
that leads to the Cessation of Suffering.
Only this Noble Eightfold Path namely,
Right Understanding, Right Intention, Right Speech,
Right Action, Right Livelihood, Right Effort,
Right Mindfulness, Right Concentration.

Dhammacakkappavattana Sutta

This Fourth Noble Truth is truly the way to spiritual liberation, because it cultivates mental balance and ease as well as the wisdom necessary to penetrate the most subtle universal truths.
The Eightfold Path is also known as the middle way, the way beyond extremes.

Bhikkhus,
there are two extremes
that should not be followed by one
who has gone forth from the worldly life, namely;
sensual indulgence, which is low, coarse,
vulgar and unprofitable, and self mortification,
which is painful, ignoble and unprofitable.
Bhikkhus, the middle path,
as understood by the Tathagata,
after he had transcended these extremes,
produces vision, produces knowledge and leads to calm,
penetration, enlightenment and Nibbana.

Dhammacakkappavattana Sutta

These were the opening remarks of the Buddha to his five
first disciples at the deer park near Benares, before he
expounded the Four Noble Truths.

The Eightfold Path

To hear the Buddha's teachings upon suffering, its cause and its cessation will bring joy to the mind of the person who realises that *'there must be more to life than this!'*
Once we understand that the struggle to control everyone and everything so that we are always happy, is futile, we begin to seek a way out of this entanglement of the mind.
The Buddhas teaching without that way, would be only a series of empty promises, pointing to a way of liberation without a clear path.
However, the Buddha as we have seen, was an eminently practical man and did not waste time in speculation, blind faith or belief. When he speaks of liberation he also speaks of the way to take us there.
This way is called the Eightfold Path.

The Buddha, whilst living in the world as a prince had experienced the extreme of sensual indulgence, a life-style where he could have anything his heart desired to make him happy, and yet had given it up because of its inherent emptiness. Even getting what he wanted could not perpetuate the feelings of happiness so eagerly sought after, for the questions of the human condition, of old age, sickness and death, would not leave him.
Living as an ascetic for six years, experiencing the life of self mortification had also not produced satisfactory results and so that too, had been renounced. Punishing the mind and body does not bring spiritual liberation and does not lead to peace. It is also unsatisfactory.

The Eightfold Path, as realised by the Buddha, should not however, be understood as a path of compromise, a way that sits happily between the two extremes of sensual indulgence and self mortification, but rather it should be understood as the transcendental path. The way beyond extremes.

The Fourth Noble Truth has eight aspects that fall into three categories of morality, mental development and wisdom.

Morality, which designates how we live in the world and can be seen as the support for the other two aspects, comprises Right Speech, Right Action and Right Livelihood.

Mental development, essential to progression along the path, comprises Right Effort, Right Mindfulness and Right Concentration.

Wisdom, the natural consequence of the first two aspects of the path, is comprised of the remaining two factors of Right Understanding and Right Intention.

Although these eight aspects manifest spontaneously moment after moment, in the traditional order of listing they follow a set pattern and it is appropriate to examine here each one in turn.

Right Understanding:

With each step of the path the word 'Right' signifies an absolute right, or a universal right, rather than right as opposed to wrong, thus transcending any mundane attitude to the path.

Right Understanding means seeing life as it really is and not clouded by our own personal interpretations, based as they are in greed, hatred and delusion.

Through the meditation process we can begin to experience for ourselves the reality of human existence, not as something substantial, beginning with birth and ending with death, but as a process emanating from a beginningless beginning and continuing towards an endless end. Nowhere in this process that includes all mental and physical phenomenon, can anything be found that does not have this changing nature. To attempt to attach to any part of this process and say, 'this is me, this is my self', brings only more unhappiness as we perpetuate our suffering through delusion.

The mind and its contents are changing in every moment. No thought, mood, feeling or emotion lasts for more than the briefest time, and so it is not possible to stop this process, even for an instant and proclaim 'this is me!'

The body also undergoes perpetual change. From the gross aspect of the aging process, carrying us from birth to death, to the sub atomic level of the momentary manifestation of the matter which constitutes it.

Nothing can be experienced that is not part of this ever changing process, a process of becoming that never becomes anything.

The Buddha summarised this most profound teaching by saying, 'All things arise and pass away, and should not be considered Self'.

At one time there was an old Brahmin who sought a teaching from the Buddha.

"Venerable Sir," he began, "I am an old man and my memory often fails me. I know that your teaching is vast, but is it possible that you can give me a short teaching so I might remember it?"

The Buddha replied, "Old man, the whole of my teaching can be expressed in one sentence, and that sentence is this; Nothing whatsoever should be clung to or grasped at as being me or mine."

Understanding that life is a constant process of change and that whatever we may think, we are not the body and we are not the mind, may be truths that can be grasped intellectually, but it is only through long hours of meditation that they can be understood intuitively. It is only this intuitive understanding that will change our relationship to life and so begin our path to true liberation.

Right Understanding also includes seeing the law of Kamma in the correct way. This law simply states that we are always responsible for our speech and actions because everything begins as an impulse of mind. When we act on this impulse we meet the consequence (*Vipaka*) of it sometime in the future.

And this is the most important thing to understand, that what we meet in every moment of our life is the consequence of that which we have empowered in the past. It is not a judgement or a punishment, it is only a consequence.

We can blame others for what they say or do, but in reality, it is always ourselves that must carry the kammic burden of our journey through this life.

The final aspect of Right Understanding concerns the Four Noble Truths themselves.

As with all teachings from the Buddha we are to consider, reflect and meditate upon what he said until we know it as a truth for ourselves, by our own direct and immediate experience.

The Four Noble Truths, concerning suffering, our experience of life, the cause of that suffering, arising as desire and craving, the cessation of that suffering, through letting go of the cause itself, and the path that leads to that cessation, the way to let go of the cause of our suffering, are truths not taught by other teachers.

The Buddha taught this path for our benefit and from compassion for our difficulties in life. It is for us to put these teachings into practice and attain the highest goal we can.

Right Intention:
The Buddha always stressed intention as the important part
of the action, rather than the outcome of the action itself. If
our intention is truly to do good and be of value to the world
by serving its needs, then the result of what we do, even if
it is not what we would have liked, is secondary to that noble
intention.

When asked the question, "Which is the worst thing, to kill
someone, to threaten to kill them or to think about killing
them?" most people would say that to kill them is the worst.
Of course this is true, but without the thought, without the
initial intention to harm, there can be no threatening speech
and no physical action.

To repeat again the teaching of Kamma from the first two
verses of the Dhammapada.

We are what we think.
All that we are arises with our mind,
and with our mind we create our world.
Speak or act with an impure mind
and difficulties will follow you,
as the wheel follows the ox
that pulls the cart.

We are what we think.
All that we are arises with our mind,
and with our mind we create our world.
Speak or act with a pure mind
and happiness will follow you
like your shadow in the brightest part of the day,
inseparable.

The surgeon who, whilst in the noble endeavor to save a

patients life on the operation table, accidentally slips with the scalpel thus causing the untimely death of that person does not carry with him the same kammic consequences as the bandit who deliberately and without compunction kills someone entirely out of greed for their possessions.

Intention is everything, and part of our Buddhist training, whether as lay person, monk or nun, is to constantly reflect on the basis of our actions, honestly examining and refining what we do and say so that all beings and not only ourselves, can benefit.

Right Speech:

To use our speech correctly is an important part of Buddhist discipline, especially when we consider that what we say is a direct reflection of our immediate mental state. Right Speech is a difficult teaching to practice for often we 'speak without thinking' or are encouraged to 'speak our mind', to say what we think without consideration for the feelings of the other person.

Right Speech in Buddhist training is speech that is gentle and kind and has the effect of harmonizing and uniting others, rather than causing further divisions amongst people. Needless to say, it should always be honest and truthful, and in this respect, silence can also be understood as the correct use of Right Speech.

Right Action:

Right Action is the way that the dedicated Buddhist will live in the world, and contains the guidelines for all physical and verbal behaviour. These guidelines, known as the 'Five Precepts', are taken voluntarily and are considered to be rules *of training*, rather than commandments insisted upon by a guiding or ruling deity.

Each of the Five Precepts begins with the phrase, 'I undertake the rule of training to ...', and then is followed by the rest of the rule, which is always one of restraint.

By not simply indulging our desires of the moment, to take or do just what we want, we allow the mental space for self examination to develop, and through that, an understanding of the nature of our unenlightened life.

The First Precept requires us to refrain from *harming any living beings.*

For a true follower of the Buddha, all life is precious, with no life form taking precedence over another. By upholding this precept we naturally become more careful about what we do, developing a more harmonious and considerate attitude towards those around us, human or not.

Strictly speaking, this precept can be understood as simply the avoidance of killing other beings, but as practicing Buddhists we can develop it much further. Not to deliberately harm any other beings through our physical action is a much more comprehensive understanding of this important rule. To live in the world in such a way that no being ever need fear us, and to develop a heart that is always ready to be of service to others.

The significance of this first training rule can be understood if we consider for a moment that if everyone in the world would agree to it, all war and animal slaughter would end immediately.

The Second Precept requires us to refrain from *taking that which has not been freely given.*

Not to steal is the obvious interpretation of this training rule and Buddhism, in keeping with all other major religious traditions, advocates respect for the property of others. However, we can develop this rule further if we begin to examine our attitudes concerning our level of patience with

This brightness cannot be experienced by a mind that is polluted by even the mildest drug or drink. This does not of course include beverages such as tea or coffee or even the now anti social habit of tobacco smoking. Nor does it include prescribed medicines.

This last precept cannot be emphasized too strongly. Drugs and alcohol destroy our self awareness and so our self discipline. Without these we cannot hope to keep the other equally important precepts or continue to advance along the path.

These then, are the lay Buddhist rules of training, the guidelines to a life-style that develops mental ease by removing the many causes of distress. By upholding these five basic principles a refinement of life can be experienced as we cease to do harm either to ourselves or others through our speech or bodily action. The resulting simplification of life brings with it such rewards as respect and trust from others as well as peace and respect from ourselves.

As with all aspects of Buddhist training we begin from where we are and no-one is expected to be perfect overnight. Mistakes are therefore a part of the growing process. However, by grounding ourselves in morality we can recognize those mistakes honestly and learn from them.

Right Livelihood:
For most of us it is not possible to dedicate ourselves completely to the Buddhist spiritual life by taking on the responsibility of the monk or nun, and so we must make our way in the world to provide for ourselves and our family.

Naturally, there is no shame or dishonour in this as each of us has his or her own kammic responsibilities to face up to. However, the way we make our living in the world is considered to be very important.

Our livelihood, supported by our moral code of conduct contained in the five precepts, should be based upon the ideal of harmlessness both to ourselves and others, and honesty, investigating our motives doing what we do. In this way we can demonstrate the Buddhas' teaching in every aspect of life. Buddhist practice is not something just to confine to temples and shrine rooms but should be reflected in everything we do. Because of this, certain occupations just by their very nature, become impossible for us to be involved in.

Traditionally, the list of unwholesome occupations contains the work of the soldier, the hunter, the fisherman, the prostitute, the money lender and the fortune teller.

The five forms of trade not to be involved in are those that deal with arms, in living beings, in flesh (there are no Buddhist butchers), and in alcohol and poisons.

By avoiding these forms of trade and livelihoods we can live in the world without the fear of guilt and shame, and so keep our life-style as pure as possible.

Of course, many of us have to make our living by working in shops and factories, and other mundane activities where there is little or no job satisfaction. However, it is our duty as followers of the Buddhist path to provide for the people we are responsible for, and even though the work itself cannot be said to be spiritually uplifting, it has value because it supports the lives of others. It is not possible for all of us to be doctors or social workers in a strong position to help others in society, but we can help those close to us. Money is an essential part of western life, without it we cannot live and so we all must work.

Right Effort:
The Buddhist practice of Right Effort can be examined in two areas.

First in general, Right effort should be considered as the effort and energy necessary to establish and then develop the spiritual life.

When all goes well for us we do not need anything special to help us along our path. Life is experienced as something pleasant and so minor inconveniences when they arise, are appreciated for their teaching quality. However, when these pleasant conditions no longer prevail and life is felt to be a drudge with no indication of ever changing we need to apply the practice of Right Effort.

To do whatever is appropriate in any given moment and not just follow our immediate desires or aversions, is how we may understand the general aspect of this part of the Eightfold Path. To sit in meditation at the appointed time even if our favorite television programme is about to begin, to hold back that cutting remark when provoked, or to offer ourselves in the service of another when we feel that we would rather do nothing, are some examples of how Right Effort can be demonstrated.

The second area of Right Effort is more particular and deals with the Buddhist practice of developing wholesome mental states at the expense of the unwholesome ones.

Technically it is divided into four parts:

Part One; The effort is generated to recognize an unwholesome mental state such as fear, greed or anger.

Part Two; The effort is generated to let go of our attachment to these unwholesome mental states and not allow them to develop further, whilst at the same time cultivating the effort to prevent further unwholesome states, not yet manifested, to grow.

Part Three; The effort is generated to recognize a wholesome mental state such as generosity, honesty or sincerity.

Part Four; The effort is generated to promote these wholesome mental states and allow them to develop, whilst at the same time cultivating the effort to promote further wholesome states, not yet manifested, to grow.

It is easy for any of us to be caught up in the stream of negative thoughts and feelings without realizing it. These mental conditions can last a long time, developing and consuming us with feelings of ill will and self doubt. These mental states are only unproductive and do not lead to peace and harmony in our lives. They have no value and need to be dismissed immediately.

The positive mental states on the other hand, do have value both to ourselves and others, allowing us to have pleasant feelings about ourselves and our relationship with the world. These states are to be encouraged and bring great benefit to our spiritual path.

The four aspects of Right Effort work together by continually recognizing, then adjusting our moods, feelings and emotions as they flow through the consciousness. This creates balance and harmony in our lives which are exactly the right conditions for our spiritual growth.

Insight, the true recognition of where all our pain and suffering really begins cannot arise from a mind that is always in conflict with itself. When we recognize that negative impulses have no value at all in the quest for perfect spiritual happiness, we can begin to focus our attention on the cultivation of the positive qualities that have real value in our lives.

These qualities are traditionally known as the Ten Perfections. They are the beautiful qualities that rest within each one of us and through practice will be released to manifest and transform our ordinary and everyday life.

The Ten Perfections are listed as follows:

GENEROSITY:
The selfless act of giving and sharing.
MORALITY:
The ability to live in the world without causing pain or harm to others.
RENUNCIATION:
Developing a more simplistic approach to life.
WISDOM:
The fruits of practice.
ENERGY:
To sustain our effort when life becomes difficult.
PATIENCE:
To be gentle with ourselves and others.
HONESTY:
The way to live without fear or guilt.
RESOLUTION:
To be determined and so see things through to their conclusion.
LOVING KINDNESS:
The way to be accepting of all beings, transcending liking and disliking.
EQUANIMITY:
To be in balance with life and so at peace with all things.

These Ten Perfections evolve and develop through practice and should not be considered as goals within themselves. They are the consequence of our efforts and can be realized by anyone who earnestly applies the teachings of the Buddha to their life.

Right Mindfulness:
Mindfulness, also called awareness is the key to development along the Buddhist path.
To recognize that all mental and physical phenomena arise

and pass away without end, and that there is no part of this process that is not subject to perpetual change and so can be truly called a 'self', is the goal of this endeavor.

The Buddhist practice used to develop this clear seeing into reality is known as *Vipassana Bhavana*, or Insight Meditation. This was the practice that had been lost to the world but was rediscovered by the Buddha, and which in turn led to his enlightenment.

The Buddhas discourse on this profound system of meditation is called the Mahasatipatthana Sutta, the great teaching on the four foundations of mindfulness.

This teaching gives comprehensive instructions as to the actual practice of meditation, and is considered to be the most important teaching after the Four Noble Truths.

The Buddha begins this sutta as follows:

Bhikkhus,
there is only one way that
leads to the purification of the minds of beings.
For the overcoming of sorrow and lamentation,
for the complete destruction of physical pain
and mental distress,
for the establishment of the Path,
and for the realization of Nibbana.
Bhikkhus,
what is this one and only way?
It is the development of awareness
into the four foundations of mindfulness.

Mahasatipatthana Sutta

The four foundations of mindfulness are then described in detail and the practitioner is advised to go to a quite place, such as a cave or the foot of a tree and practice until he attains his final goal.

These days it may not be possible for many of us to go into solitude and practice Insight Meditation, but even in our daily lives, occupied with our usual activities, we can expect good results if we apply ourselves.

The four foundations are areas where we can apply investigative awareness or mindfulness. These areas are, the body, the feelings, the mind and the changing contents of the mind.

By turning our attention to these four areas we can realize the fundamental truth of impermanence for ourselves.

Nothing is outside the process of change, so any attachment to any part of it as being me or mine, can only lead to the experience of unhappiness and perpetuate our suffering.

Right Concentration:

If Right Mindfulness is the only way to the realization of the truth, then Right Concentration is the only way to the attainment of Right Mindfulness.

Concentration, or more correctly, *One Pointedness of Mind*, is the essential ingredient for not only developing the meditation practice of awareness, but also for bringing focus and attention into our daily life.

In ordinary life our degree of focus or concentration is diffused into the myriad forms of distractions that bombard our senses, leaving us jaded, dull and exhausted by the end of the day. By applying Right Concentration in harmony with Right Effort and Right Mindfulness, we can determine the quality of our thoughts, moods, feelings and emotions and retain those worthy of further consideration whilst quickly disregarding those we consider to be unwholesome or unproductive.

This process becomes more and more spontaneous through

practice and the ensuing results bring a greater level of peace into our lives, and the ability to respond to external pressures comfortably.

Within the practice of Insight Meditation, Right Mindfulness cannot be brought fully into play until Right Concentration has been firmly established.

The importance of Right Concentration cannot be over emphasized. It is the basis for all Buddhist meditation practice and is the fundamental principle of a more peaceful and harmonious life.

Thus we have the essence of the teaching of the Buddha.

The Four Noble Truths, revealing our suffering, its cause, its cessation and the Eightfold Path, the way that leads to its cessation.

The Eightfold Path manifests moment after moment and in every aspect of our lives. It is not contained in a special place or only available at a special time. This path is available for us in every moment of our lives and so we have always the opportunity to walk it. To cultivate our morality, our mental development and our wisdom, and so truly immerse ourselves in the teaching of the Buddha.

This way of practice is a fundamental aspect of Buddhist training, a way that emphasizes not a belief in books, tradition, words or ideas, but a direct experience of the Truth of our own existence.

However, it is for us to apply ourselves at every instant and make the best use of this wonderful opportunity as a human being to realize our perfect potential for enlightenment.

You yourselves must make the effort,
Buddhas only point the way.
Those who practice serenity and insight meditation
are freed from the bonds
of ignorance.

Dhammapada: verse 276

Walking the Path

Walking the Path

Part two

Walking the Path

Walking the Path

Having briefly looked at the early life and fundamental teachings of the Buddha, we now turn our attention to the application of these teachings within the confines of our usual everyday
Western lives.

In Buddhist countries throughout the world the social roles of monastic and lay person are clearly defined, with neither needing to ask the other about appropriate behaviour. However in the West, with our own culture and social graces developed from strictly non Buddhist sources, we may feel at a loss when, on the one hand due to our faith and conviction in the teaching of the Buddha we want to respond to circumstances in a purely Buddhist way, whilst on the other hand, due to our social conditioning, we hesitate to do anything.

How to be a Buddhist in the West is a profound question for many people living in our society. What are our spiritual obligations towards individuals and the community and what duties are we expected to perform? Where should we begin to demonstrate our conviction towards Buddhist teachings and what guidelines can we follow?

As we have already seen, Buddhism is a way of profound personal development. The teaching of the law of Kamma demonstrates that. Our place within the teaching is to bring ourselves to perfection and not expect others to be perfect for us. To live a blameless life is our target and to put our spiritual development above all things.

Without reflection this may sound a selfish way to live, but in fact the opposite is true. Until we are able to live spontaneously in the world with love and wisdom, we surely only help to contribute to the confusion, pain and suffering that already abounds. One more ignorant being doing everything they can to make the world a perfect place for themselves!

> By oneself unwholesome actions are made,
> and by oneself one suffers.
> By oneself wholesome actions are made,
> and by oneself one is purified.
> Purity and impurity depend entirely upon oneself,
> no-one can purify another.

> Dhammapada: verse 165

The foundation of our action in the world is our attitude of morality and the development of virtue. This is encapsulated by our intention to always live within the guidelines of the five precepts. These precepts it is said, is how the enlightened being spontaneously lives.

By endeavouring to fulfil these five training rules we no longer simply act out of desire or aversion, but rather do what is appropriate in each situation. To follow the loving heart rather than the desiring head.

The restraining of speech or action that has no value or beneficial effect within the home or society in general, can be considered the corner stone to our own personal development, and a blessing to the situation.

However, if we are committed to upholding the basic moral precepts of Buddhism we will often experience confusion and even resistance to them as our understanding grows into maturity. Probing and examining through meditation and contemplation what was once thought to be fully understood, now becomes a question again and requires an answer. An answer this time not from the intellect, but from the intuitive understanding of the truth.

In everyday circumstances our understanding of the Buddhas teaching is challenged and new opportunities for development along the path can be cultivated and brought to fruition.

For example, if we find ourselves in a situation where, for whatever reason, we want to give someone a 'piece of our mind', and tell them in no uncertain circumstance exactly what we think of them, we can apply the Buddhist teaching. In this instance we have to remember our determination to uphold the fourth precept concerning wrong speech and the third step of the Eightfold Path, concerning Right Speech and so keep unwholesome views and opinions, as well as insulting language to ourselves. This also provides the opportunity to examine our feelings and to bring into that moment the practice of Right Effort, letting go of unwholesome mental states and allowing wholesome mental states to replace them. This example would also allow the development of compassion and loving kindness towards that person whilst the whole incident would be supported by Right Concentration and Right Mindfulness.

So here we have an everyday occurrence where with diligence and attention we can apply many aspects of the teaching in a natural and spontaneous way, thus allowing for the continuing development of wisdom and peace.

When we understand in the right way, we see that our Buddhist path is a living path and relevant to every situation.

The five precepts are our everyday guide to general behaviour and with continued application will form the natural base for our life-style. However, in certain circumstances it will be appropriate for us to uphold more than these simple training rules. On the occasion of a visit to a Buddhist monastery or vihara, for a day or even longer (as in the case of a meditation retreat for example) we will be required to keep extra rules of training.

The Eight Precepts:

The eight precepts consist of our usual five with three extra rules added to them. They now become:

I undertake the rule of training to refrain from harming any living beings.

I undertake the rule of training to refrain from taking that which is not freely given.

I undertake the rule of training to refrain from any sexual misconduct.

I undertake the rule of training to refrain from the use of wrong speech.

I undertake the rule of training to refrain from drinks and drugs that cloud the mind.

I undertake the rule of training to refrain from taking untimely meals.

I undertake the rule of training to refrain from dancing, singing and music and watching grotesque mime and from the use of garlands, perfumes, cosmetics and personal adornments.

I undertake the rule of training to refrain from the use of high beds.

These extra precepts require some explanation.

The life of the Buddhist monk or nun is an extremely simple one, being entirely dependent on the generosity of the lay community. In order for this generosity to arise the monks and nuns must be seen to live pure lives and so be worthy of alms. They must also be modest in their requirements and this includes food. The Buddha established the sixth precept rule against the taking of untimely meals so that his monastic followers would not be seen to be spending considerable parts of the day acquiring and consuming food. This means that the demands on the laity would be minimal.

The sixth precept also dictates that all food, having been offered and then collected by the monastic order, should be eaten by noon of that day and that no further food should be consumed until after the dawn of the next day. No food is to be stored.

All monks and nuns, especially of the Theravada tradition adhere to this rule although in most monasteries in Europe a light breakfast of gruel is served. However, the main meal of the day is lunch and always eaten before noon.

One very senior monk now residing in England was travelling across Europe by aeroplane on one occasion and due to circumstances beyond his control, was not able to take his meal before the prescribed time. Rather than break this important precept he fasted until the next day, such was his determination to keep intact this important precept.

As lay people spending time in monasteries and viharas, we too must show our determination to uphold this particular rule of training. It is important for us to remember that all food consumed on these premises has been bought or grown, cooked and offered by devout lay supporters for those undergoing any kind of Buddhist training.

To us as Westerners, with our full refrigerators and even fuller stomachs, it may seem like an impossible task to survive from noon to dawn the next day without something to eat, however in practice most people suffer more with the idea of light fasting than with the reality of it. In fact, due to taking less food than usual they find that they have a higher level of energy to direct towards their meditation practice and listening to the teachings.

The seventh precept is a very long one but in simple terms it means that we should turn our attention away from the usual distractions we find in everyday life such as dancing and singing, theatre and now of course television and radio and focus inward to the task of spiritual development. This precept is really just a simplification of our usual life-style and also includes restraint from the wearing of perfume and jewellery so that we are not just wasting our efforts in acts of self adornment and vanity.

It is the removal of these many distractions that leads to deeper and more revealing depths of understanding about ourselves. As with all the rules of training, it is by resisting our habits and almost unconscious desires that we can discover their power over us and so take ourselves out, perhaps for the first time, of the position of being the victim to them.

Not to use high beds may sound unusual for us in the West, as beds off the floor are the rule rather than the exception. However, although this precept does not mean that we all have to sleep on the carpet, it does mean that we have to be careful with regard to our indulgence in luxury.

On meditation retreats or shorter stays in monasteries and viharas, our minds should be turned to the business at hand, that is developing the spiritual side of our nature, without worrying whether our chair is comfortable enough or our bed is as good as the one at home. On meditation retreats in particular, whatever difficulties or discomforts arise can be considered as objects for reflection and not obstacles to enlightenment.

This rule is also understood as one of humility.

In the time of the Buddha only high ranking people would have high beds in their homes and so it was considered to be a position of authority. However, in the monastery, no matter what position we may hold in society, it means nothing. On our spiritual journey we are all equal and the only thing that will truly help us to walk this path, is wisdom.

These three extra training rules are undertaken for our own benefit. By following them to the best of our ability we are able to refine our life and our behaviour so that we do not disturb those around us and do not make excessive demands on those who support us. On every occasion when the eight precepts are taken, the third precept concerning indulgence in the sensory world changes to a rule of celibacy. No sexual contact of any kind is allowable.

In traditional Buddhist countries the days on which the four quarters of the moon fall are seen as the times when special effort can be made and the eight precepts can be taken. In monasteries there will be chanting and extra teachings from the monks, as well as all night communal meditation. This is considered to be an important activity for lay people or not only does it develop a strong determination to progress along the spiritual path, but it is also seen as a good way to develop merit.

Problems and Difficulties

May all beings without exception, be happy.

Metta Sutta

A problem increasingly common in the West is that of conflicting spiritual values between partners involved in a lasting relationship. Many Westerners find that whilst they want to consider themselves Buddhists and apply the teachings to their daily lives, even to the point of upholding the eight precepts on moon days, rather than developing a harmonious atmosphere in the home, it leads to conflict and argument. The other person then begins to see Buddhist practice not as something that can bring peace and understanding into life, but as something divisive. Something that separates them from the person they were close to. The activity of solitary meditation and not eating after noon or going to see a show on the moon days are considered excessive and leads to a feeling of isolation and separateness within the relationship. Naturally argument and upset arise from this situation and neither party feels very much happiness from Buddhist practice.

This is a familiar story told to Buddhist monks living in the West by unhappy Western Buddhists. In short, my partner doesn't understand my practice - what can I do?

The answer is always the same.

As Buddhists it is our duty to consider our family and loved ones first in all things. We have our obligation to provide them with the necessary requirements of life, such as food, clothing and education, as well as maintaining to the best of our ability, a harmonious and stable home environment. Our purpose has to be to develop the potential of the family as a path to enlightenment, and not see it as a hindrance to practice.

Of course, if we consider ourselves as lay Buddhists, it is for us to take the lead in moral and spiritual concerns, but this must be done from the front. That is to say, by example. We must treat all beings with kindness and respect and understand that each one of us is responding to the world with different degrees of understanding. It is not for us to condemn others out of hand because they can't see things our way. In normal family relationships everyone has their respective duties to perform and it is unfair and unreasonable of us to have expectations of others that they cannot live up to.

As Buddhists this must be the attitude we must adopt. Our first intention must be to develop a loving caring atmosphere within the family and then, without excluding, isolating or worse, preaching, encourage by our own attitudes the development of a more spiritual environment.

In some situations there will be hostility and ridicule to spiritual development. In others it may not be the case.

One thing we can know for certain is that everything is always changing and as Buddhists we can respond to those changes in the most harmonious way, and use them as opportunities for spiritual growth.

In Buddhist countries, men and women attend meditation courses at a time when their lives are most congenial, thus enhancing the happiness that is already established. In the West, the opposite is true. Westerners tend to visit these places at the times when there is the most trouble and turmoil in their lives, looking for the secret to happiness.

We have to literally put *our own house in order* first, and not seek to avoid family obligations by immersing ourselves in a spiritual practice that is just an escape from our responsibilities.

The purpose of the Buddhas' teaching is to bring understanding and wisdom into our lives, so that ultimately, all beings can benefit from our presence.

The Ten Precepts:
From eight precepts we now move to ten.
The taking of ten precepts is mainly for samaneras, men or young boys waiting for full ordination, very devout lay people who are able to live away from their family and work situations for long periods, and Theravadin nuns.
Although an order of Buddhist nuns was established by the Buddha in Theravada countries this has now died out and due to complex initiation procedures, cannot easily be re-established. However, any woman seeking ordination can live as a 'ten preceptor', and experience the nuns life fully by upholding these rules. Dedication, determination and devotion are the cornerstones to practice and spiritual development, not the number of rules kept.
By creating ten precepts, certain changes are brought to the already existing eight.
The seventh precept now divides into two parts and so becomes;

I undertake the rule of training to refrain from dancing, singing, music and watching grotesque mime.

Whilst the eighth precept is made up of the rest;

I undertake the rule of training to refrain from the use of garlands, perfumes and personal adornments.

The ninth precept is now concerned with the use of high beds, while the only new precept applies to the handling of money.

I undertake the rule of training to refrain from using gold or silver.

At the time of the Buddha, as with now, one thing was seen as being of absolute importance, and that was the dependency of the monastic order on the laity.

The monks and nuns were to own very little (traditionally only eight items) and were not allowed to be self sufficient. This meant that their life, as simple as it was, needed the constant support of the lay community. For this to be feasible, the conduct of the monks and nuns needed to be as pure as possible, thus setting a standard of morality and conduct for the lay person to aspire to, and themselves be worthy of alms support. This generates mutual respect and trust, as the monastics provide the example of excellence and spiritual teachings for social and cultural based events, whilst the lay community provides the material requirements.

However, this balance could be easily upset if a monk or nun had access to a private income and so was not wholly dependent on the lay generosity. In this instance what need had they to lead a life of example if they always had enough money to feed and clothe themselves? For this reason the Buddha established the tenth precept, the rule of poverty.

The ten precepts are the most a lay man or woman can take. The next level of training in the Buddhist tradition is for men only and requires a quantum leap from ten to two hundred and twenty seven training rules.

This is called the Patimokkha, the disciplines concerning the comportment and conduct of a monk.

It is said that for the first twenty five years of the Buddhas teaching, no training rules were necessary because all his followers quickly became established on the path of enlightenment, to at least the first level, called stream enterer. Once established here it is impossible for anyone to fall back into the ways of the world and so their moral conduct was always exemplary with no need of guiding rules. However, as time progressed many ordinary worldly men and women became attracted to the monastic life, perhaps not always for the purest of reasons. Possibly they saw it as a life of relative ease allowing a degree of respect not usually offered to them. However, whatever advantage they saw in giving up the home life for the homeless one, because of their wrong intention, infringements in the intuitively recognized code of moral conduct began to occur.

Although it may sound contrary, the Buddha was not a man to make lists of rules for no adequate reason. The first rule appeared only after the first transgression and the transgressor was not punished but reminded of his folly. However, once the rule was established it became law in the community.

The two hundred and twenty seven rules governing the behavior of Buddhist monks are taken very seriously and although the minor ones can be adapted to suit different cultures and conditions, generally they are held intact according to the Buddhas instruction.

The Patimokkha is recited once every two weeks in the monasteries of the Theravada tradition and so keeps the teachings of conduct and discipline alive in the monastic community.

The precepts then are the way that the lay Buddhist relates his or her behaviour to the rest of society, either individually or *en masse*, and as we have seen function on different levels for different occasions. Therefore, whatever the situation, a comprehensive guide to conduct can be depended upon.

We can now look at the other responsibilities and commitments that the statement 'I am a Buddhist', implies.

Because Buddhism is not part of our social and cultural background there are many occasions when we would like to uphold fully Buddhist principles, but in effect just don't know what to do. Buddhism as an ideal is not the same as Buddhism in practice.

Of course it can be said that an enormous contribution is already being made to society by anyone keeping the five precepts. By no longer blindly acting from desire and hatred, but by reflecting and taking wise action appropriate to the situation, we already give much to the betterment of all. Even in this small practice of morality we stop adding to the fears, suspicions, anxieties and general mistrust that abounds in modern society, but create an oasis of peace in our honesty, uprightness and openness.

However, if we truly do consider ourselves to be lay Buddhists and wish to fulfil an active role in society, we need to reflect and consider how we can best serve those around us.

Walking the Path

Walking the Path

Part Three

Walking the Path

The Ten Wholesome Actions

One should not think lightly of doing good,
imagining 'a little will not affect me',
for just as a water jar is filled by falling drops of rain,
so too is the wise one filled with merit,
by accumulating little by little.

Dhammapada: verse 122

It has been said that Buddhism is a selfish religion concerned only with the spiritual liberation of the individual. However, by turning our attention to the Ten Wholesome Actions we can see that this is not the case and in fact the opposite is true.

It is the obligation of any Buddhist monk or nun, layman or laywoman to strive earnestly for their own liberation, but at the same time working within society to help, teach, be of service and ultimately provide the circumstances whereby all beings will benefit and so live better, happier and more harmonious lives.

The Ten Wholesome Actions are:

GENEROSITY
MORALITY
MENTAL CULTURE
REVERENCE
SERVICE
TRANSFERENCE OF MERIT
REJOICING IN THE MERIT OF OTHERS
HEARING THE DHAMMA
TEACHING THE DHAMMA
CORRECTING THE WRONG VIEWS OF OTHERS

These ten actions can be seen as being of service to others, whilst at the same time helping us to develop our own practice.

Like two hands that wash each other. We help others and it is by helping others that we help ourselves.

Generosity

At one time the King Pasenadi of Kosala made a generous offering to the Buddha. His subjects on hearing this also wanted to make an offering and so organised an alms giving ceremony to out do the king.

When the king heard this he made an even grander gesture of generosity to out do his subjects, and so it went on. Each time the king gave alms to the Buddha, his subjects responded by giving more. The king then felt obliged to offer even more. Neither side would rest until the other admitted defeat. The Kings' wife Queen Mallika eventually devised a plan to show once and for all who was the greatest at offering alms to the Buddha.

She told her husband to organise an alms giving ceremony on such a huge scale that it would be impossible for the people to compete. This ceremony involved the building of a pavilion large enough to house five hundred white elephants that would hold five hundred white umbrellas over the heads of five hundred monks. Also, at the centre of the pavilion would be ten barges filled with perfume and incense and two hundred and fifty princesses to fan the five hundred monks. It would be unbeatable!

On the day of the ceremony, food was offered to the Buddha and his retinue as well as everything contained within the pavilion, which now had a value of fourteen crores, a huge amount of money.

At that time two ministers of the king were present. The first named Junha, was pleased and delighted with the kings great display of generosity towards the Buddha and his monks. He recognised that such an offering could only be made by a great king and that all beings would benefit because of it. The second minister, called Kala, held the opposite view. He felt that this was just a huge waste of money and the monks would only eat everything offered to them and go back to their monasteries and sleep.

After the meal the Buddha, realising the mental state of Kala, gave only a short dhamma talk and returned to his monastery. King Pasenadi however, was disappointed that the Buddha had spoken only a little and felt that perhaps he had failed to do something and the Buddha had taken this as a mark of disrespect. With his mind troubled he followed the Buddha back to the monastery.

When the Buddha saw the king he recognised his mental state immediately and told him that he should be happy to make such an offering. Not only that, but this opportunity would arise only once during the appearance of an enlightened being. He also told the king that he knew Kalas' view on the matter and that if he had given a longer discourse in honour of the alms ceremony it would only increase his resentment and dissatisfaction and as a consequence, increase his suffering in this life and the next.

"Great King, it is fools that do not rejoice in the generosity of others and so go to the lower worlds. The wise do rejoice in the generosity of others and so, through appreciation accumulate merit and go to the world of the gods."

He then spoke in verse as follows:

Indeed misers do not go to the abodes of the gods,
fools do not praise generosity.
The wise rejoice in generosity
and so gain happiness in the life hereafter.

Dhammapada: verse 117

The acts of giving and sharing are highly praised by all

Buddhists and references to the benefits of generosity can be found throughout the scriptures. For the one who delights in giving, such benefits are; long life, good appearance, happiness and strength. Other benefits are; gaining the respect of others, association with worthy people, good reputation, self confidence and a good rebirth. Therefore we can safely assume that it is within our best interests to develop a giving heart. However, we should understand that it is not the gift itself, or even the act of giving that carries with it the prime importance, but the intention behind the act. To give for the wrong reason, even though the actual gift itself is beneficial to the recipient, will not carry with it the same kammically wholesome result that one can expect from a gift given free from any sense of expectation of something in return. Even a 'thank you', if required by the giver transforms the act of giving into a barter, '*I will give you this, but you must give me something in return*'. Naturally, this cannot be considered 'pure giving', in the Buddhist sense, coming from an egoless mind.

Generosity is regarded as the basis for all selfless action, to give and share for the benefit of others, and is not only the first of the Ten Wholesome Actions but also the first in the list of the Ten Perfections.

But we also have to use wisdom in our generosity. To give away all our material possessions on a sudden whim shows no wisdom at all. We need to provide for ourselves and our families. Once we have done this we are in a position to give to others and share what we have. If we don't have anything, what is there to share?

In the East of course, there is a long tradition of offerings being made to 'holy men'. This is understood as a way for the lay supporter to make merit by helping another human being, especially someone walking the path of Dhamma. Someone worthy.

In the Buddhist tradition this is most clearly represented by the morning alms round where the monks, in a single, silent line, walk from house to house in order to collect their food for the day. The lay supporters give to the monks freely knowing that they will not even receive a 'thank you' or other acknowledgement for their kindness. The giving is done in silence and the receiving is done in silence. The beautiful action allows the laity the opportunity to participate in pure giving. Giving without any thought of receiving something in return.

There are many ways in which we can give, but each way should be seen as an aspect of practice coming from a mind not tainted by the effects of ego and selfishness, no matter how subtle. The Buddha advises us, 'Never hesitate to do good', for in that very hesitation all the easily justifiable reasons for not doing anything arise and an opportunity is lost. We loose and the person needing our help looses also.

Each opportunity for giving to others whether materially or from ourselves in the way of time, a helping hand or a listening ear, should be seen as a chance to develop both our heart and our Buddhist understanding.

The ultimate form of giving can be found in the Buddhist scriptures where humans and animals have offered their lives so that others can live.

At one time there was a sage living a life of solitude in the hills, spending his time meditating and reflecting on the Dhamma. One day whilst wandering alone he came across a tigress and her newly born litter of cubs.

The tigress was lying on her side with her cubs gathered around her crying and complaining because there was no milk for them.

It was a sad and sorry sight, for through a long and difficult delivery, the tigress had exhausted herself and now had no strength to hunt. As the days passed she had grown weaker and weaker and her milk had run dry. Now the whole family faced a slow and painful death through starvation.

The sage assessed the situation and realised that there was only one thing he could do. In an act of pure selflessness and disregarding his own interests completely, he took out his knife and offered his life so that they might live.

The tigress first smelt the fresh blood next to her and with some effort was able to taste some. During the course of the next few days, thanks to the ultimate act of generosity by the sage, the tigress was able to gather her strength and feed her cubs. In time finally the family were able to leave the place where the sage had given his life for them, leaving only his bones bleaching in the sun*.

This story may present an extreme form of generosity, and probably none of us will ever have to offer up our lives to save another, but the message is clear. Generosity, the act of giving and sharing whatever we have with other beings, is the noblest of acts, and when tempered with wisdom is a true step on the Buddhist path.

*Jataka Tales - stories of the previous lives of the Buddha, often as animals.

Morality

At one time the venerable Sariputta, one of the Buddha's chief disciples, visited his home village of Nalaka with many other monks to collect alms food. During the alms round he stood at the door of his mothers house and waited silently with eyes downcast for an offer that might be made.

His mother, upon seeing and recognising Sariputta invited all the monks into her home, but as she was offering the food she began to scold her son, saying, "Oh you eater of scraps, you have given up your great wealth and shamed us all!" She then continued to pour scorn on all the monks present, accusing them of using her son just to get food for that day.

Sariputta said nothing but mildly left the house and returned to the monastery.

Later, the other monks told the Buddha about the incident and how Venerable Sariputta had borne his mothers abuse and not reacted.

To them the Buddha replied that wise men never become angry and never loose their temper.

Then the Buddha spoke in verse as follows:

> Him I call a wise man who is free from anger,
>> who cultivates moral behaviour,
>> is virtuous and free from desires,
>> who is controlled in his senses.
>> For him, this existence is his last.

Dhammapada: verse 400

So much has already been said about the importance of the practice and continued refinement of Buddhist morality, that it is not necessary to repeat it here. However, certain considerations should be borne in mind.

Buddhist morality needs to be ultimately, a natural morality arising from a pure heart, not forced or imposed upon ourselves or others. It should be understood that moral behaviour is the foundation of all mental development and consequently, our right attitude towards it is paramount.

Our moral attitude needs to be established in an intention to create a life-style that carries with it an atmosphere of peace and harmony, wherever we may be. There should be no sense of strain or teeth gritting pressure to live under a particular regime of purity, and absolutely no demands on others that they conform to our ideas of social or moral conduct.

Spiritual development on whatever level, is a completely personal process, and it is not for us to condemn or even discuss the perceived failings of others.

We have here very much the idea of live and let live.

The five, eight or ten precepts are considered as training rules, something to be applied to our life for our benefit, and not god given commandments that are to be obeyed for fear of divine retribution.

We uphold the precepts to improve the situation for ourselves, and then, by extension, for all beings that we come into contact with. In Buddhist practice no-one is expected to be perfect immediately, but our goal should be to develop ourselves, little by little until perfect morality becomes our natural way of life.

> The one who always finds fault with others
> will allow his own faults to grow,
> and is far, far away from purity.

> Dhammapada: verse 253

Mental Culture

At one time a certain farmer lost an ox. Having spent all day looking for it, he finally arrived at a small Buddhist monastery that evening. The farmer was invited in by the monks and offered some food which was the remains of their mid-day meal. It was whilst eating this small meal that the farmer reflected that even working all day he could never expect to eat as well as this. It was then he decided that the best thing for him would be to abandon farming and become a monk.

This he did and in fact soon put on weight, but before too long he tired of the monks life and yearned to be a lay man again. He disrobed and returned to his family and farm. However, the work was as hard as ever and he quickly became dissatisfied and once again took the robe and became a monk.

This happened six times in all, until eventually the monks and the family of the farmer became tired of his coming and going.

During his last stay with his family he walked into the bedroom one night to see his heavily pregnant wife asleep on the bed. She was almost naked as the cover had slipped off her and she was snoring loudly with saliva trickling down her chin. Thus seeing her open mouth and bloated belly the farmer reflected upon the unwholesomeness of his wife's body and how as she lay there asleep she looked exactly like a corpse. It was in this moment of reflection that he came to understand completely the unwholesome and unsatisfactory nature of the body. With this thought in mind he picked up his monks saffron robe and headed back to the monastery for the seventh time.

The monks at first refused to admit him, being dubious of his intentions, but eventually complied with his wishes. After only a few days of devoting himself fully to the monks life of morality and meditation he attained enlightenment.

The other monks soon became curious when he no longer yearned for his old life-style, as he has done so often in the past, and asked him outright what had brought about this change of heart.

To this he replied that before his enlightenment he was driven by his attachments first here, then there, but now he was no longer attached to anything and so was at peace.

Some of the monks could not believe this claim and so reported the matter to the Buddha. The Buddha answered them by saying that what the farmer had told them was the truth and his previous behaviour of moving from his farm to the monastery and back again was because his mind was not steadfast, and so he had not understood the truth of reality. However, now as an enlightened being he fully comprehended the truth of reality and had completely let go of both good and evil.

The Buddha then spoke in verse as follows:

If a mans mind is unsteady,
if he is ignorant of the truth
and his confidence is wavering,
his knowledge will never be perfect.

If a mans mind is free from passion,
if he is free from ill will,
if he has let go of both good and evil,
and is vigilant,
then for such a man there is no danger.

Dhammapada: verses 38 & 39

For many years now people in the West have been becoming more and more aware of their own physical nature with a strong emphasis placed on diet, exercise and an all round healthy life-style. Jogging, aerobics, general sporting activities and attention to weight and appearance have all gained an importance hitherto unknown in our society. However, the development of a mind able to penetrate the more subtle truths of human existence, manifesting the qualities of balance and peace has not been given the same importance. We may all look good on the outside but what is really happening within?

From the Buddhist perspective this is most definitely 'putting the cart before the horse'.

To quote again the first two verses of the Dhammapada:

We are what we think.
All that we are arises with our mind,
and with our mind we create our world.
Speak or act with an impure mind
and difficulties will follow you,
as the wheel follows the ox
that pulls the cart.

We are what we think.
All that we are arises with our mind,
and with our mind we create our world.
Speak or act with a pure mind
and happiness will follow you
like your shadow in the brightest part of the day,
inseparable.

Dhammapada: verses 1&2

From these two verses we can see quite clearly the importance placed by Buddhists on the development of mind as the means to supreme happiness in our lives.

It is the mind that dictates our relationship to ourselves, others and the world that we live in. Only through our continual refinement of our usual mental states based as they are in greed, hatred and delusion, can we hope to attain the complete and perfect peace that is Nibbana.

The Buddha tells us that this goal is realizable in this very lifetime, and it is with the reach of all who will walk the path.

Meditation as the way to mental culture:

The Buddha taught forty different subjects for meditation, depending on the character and personality of the practitioner. Each technique is suitable for the removal of certain taints or obstructions hindering the practitioner in attaining the final goal of Nibbana.

Of these forty different types however, only three were considered suitable for all meditators and are not dependent on individual personality dispositions.

These three practices are:

Mindfulness of Breathing (Anapanasati)
Insight Meditation (Vipassana Bhavana)
Loving Kindness (Metta Bhavana)

The prolonged cultivation of these three simple practices, forming as they do the basis of the dedicated and determined lay disciples daily meditation routine, bring about deep and lasting changes in our usual mental habits by revealing the cause of our suffering or unhappiness and the wisdom to know what to do about it.

Intellectual development although important, is never considered the means to cultivate an understanding of our fundamental reality. We only arrive at more thinking. More thoughts and more concepts. To truly penetrate the truth of our existence we have to go beyond the intellectual mind to the intuitive. The mind beyond the thinking, judging and rationalizing processes. To achieve this, we must meditate.

All meditation begins with posture. The Buddha advised us to develop awareness of ourselves, no matter what posture we assume, whether sitting, standing, walking or lying down. However, when we consider formal meditation practice we tend to regard a seated posture as correct. No doubt we have all seen the statues and pictures of the Buddha with his legs neatly folded, one on top of the other, meditating or teaching in the posture known as the 'full lotus'. A less extreme form of this posture is the half lotus where only one leg is folded onto the top of the other. Both these postures are correct for meditation though neither is compulsory. There are many positions we can assume for formal meditation practice, from simply sitting cross legged on a cushion (like an old fashioned tailor), kneeling posture to even sitting western style on a chair. The purpose of correct posture is to maintain the body in a state of relative stillness for a prearranged period of time. With the body still and quiet the mind can get on with the work in hand without worrying about such trivial things as physical comfort. Of course sometimes, especially in the early days of practice many things will distract us from our meditation object such as aches and pains and itches, and movement may become necessary, but this should always be kept to a minimum and always used as an integral part of training.

By keeping any movements as slow and as mindful as possible

we can maintain our awareness and so not interrupt our focus or concentration. Simple acts such as scratching an itch or relieving an aching limb take on a whole new depth of meaning as we begin to develop the meditative habit.

Posture then is important, but entirely personal. The only conditions that apply to all meditators are that the back should be straight, though relaxed and not tense, and the head and neck should be balanced easily on the shoulders. The rest depends on you, your body and your personal preference.

Mindfulness of Breathing
Anapanasati

Having experimented and found the posture most suitable for our own body we can proceed to the actual practice of meditation itself. The initial part of our meditation 'sit', is to develop the concentration or focus, necessary to obtain maximum results. For this we use Mindfulness of Breathing. Concentration or more accurately, 'One Pointedness of Mind', is the gentle yet persistent focusing of our attention away from the everyday objects of the senses, and towards the particular subject of meditation, in this instance the breathing process. By giving ourselves to this practice a heightened yet calm and peaceful awareness is established. This awareness can be maintained for long periods, and when fully developed through practice, is no longer disturbed by intrusions from the everyday events that take place around us.

We can say that usually our mind runs freely first here, then there, constantly seeking new interest in the things around it through the senses of touch, taste, sight, hearing and smell, to ideas, emotions, memories of the past and plans for the future, it roams without restraint in a continual battle to thwart boredom. Finally, when there is nothing left to interest it, or it has become exhausted through its dizzy pursuit for stimulation, it sleeps, but still, never really resting. Even here it realises its' confusion as dreams, and preparation for the first waking moment.

This, very simply put, is the nature of the mind, and it is this very nature we have to confront during the practice of mindfulness of breathing. The Buddhist scriptures tell us that concentration is hard to understand, much less develop, and as we sit, trying to focus our attention during the first minutes of meditation practice, we will experience directly this busy and ever roaming mind. The Buddha himself reminds us that it is easier to tame a wild animal than to train this mind of ours.

The most important aspect to understand about the practice of Mindfulness of Breathing concerns the actual movement of breath.

There are many meditation techniques where the breath is controlled in some way, to inhale for a certain number of counts, to hold the breath after the inhalation, and to exhale for another, sometimes longer number of counts.

This is certainly not the practice of Mindfulness of Breathing. Our body knows how to breathe. We do not need to instruct it or interfere with it, and whether we are awake or asleep, drunk or sober, the breath goes on by itself. In this technique, the breath must not be controlled in any way, and the body must be allowed to breathe, at its own natural rate and rhythm.

Having settled ourselves in a suitable posture, we close our eyes and rest our attention at the nostrils and allow ourselves to become focused on this small area of our body.

We begin to become aware of the movement of breath with each inhalation and each exhalation as it passes through the nasal passage, by remaining at the place where the sensation of breath is felt most strongly. Our concentration and awareness begins to develop by continuing with this practice, and we cultivate a calm and dispassionate attitude and clarity into the whole of the breathing.

We become aware of the nature of breath, if it is long or short, deep or shallow, fast or slow, and with this awareness, based upon the development of a 'one pointed mind', comes a sense of detachment that results in the experience of calmness and peace.

Of course there will be many distractions both physical and mental, but with the technique of Mindfulness of Breathing, we simply turn our attention away from them as soon as they are noticed, and return to the sensation of breath in the nostrils. Eventually these distractions fall away and leave us with the peacefulness and mental sharpness that is ready for the next stage of meditation practice.

Insight Meditation
Vipassana Bhavana

Insight meditation is unique to the Buddhist tradition of spiritual development, and was the system discovered and used by the Buddha himself to gain his own enlightenment. Its importance as the ultimate vehicle to self realization cannot be overstressed, and the Buddha outlines this importance in a famous sutta.

Bhikkhus,
there is only one way that
leads to the purification of the minds of beings,

for the overcoming of sorrow and lamentation,
for the complete destruction of physical pain
and mental distress,
for the establishment of the Path,
and for the realization of Nibbana.
Bhikkhus,
what is this one and only way?
It is the development of awareness
into the four foundations of mindfulness.

Mahasatipatthana Sutta

The Buddha then goes on to describe and analyse the Four Foundations of Mindfulness, now also known as Insight Meditation, beginning with Mindfulness of Breathing.

The four centres or bases, where mindfulness can be established are; the body, mental feelings (pleasant, unpleasant or neutral), sensory consciousness and mental states. To apply sustained awareness to one or all of these areas will bring about deep and significant changes in our lives, and will eradicate the delusion of a permanent soul or self as the truth of our existence is revealed.

Insight Meditation is the technique of developing a heightened awareness of all mental and physical activity. Within the framework of a calm and peaceful mind, developed through the practice of Mindfulness of Breathing, we can directly experience our own mental and physical condition as it manifests moment after moment.

Without choosing one thing over another, we are able to see and understand the real nature of this mind and body, and know that everything continually arises and passes away in an endless stream. All our thoughts, moods, feelings and emotions are nothing more than this continuing process, and our liberation in life comes the intuitive understanding that this process is not what we are, but rather something we can be aware of.

Through the practice of Insight Meditation, we will know that anger is simply anger, and not only that, it only ever has the power that we give it. It is the same with fear, depression, anxiety and all mind states. They are like clouds that pass through the sky, seemingly real but actually empty of any real substance. When we do not empower these mind states, they cannot stay.

To know the mind in this way is to no longer be a victim to it, and the way to peace is to accept everything it offers graciously and to let go of our attachment to it. We understand the reality of our existence as we recognise that the mind is a never-ending process of beginnings and endings, but never what we are.

As this is not meant to be a manual of Insight Meditation,* there is no need here to venture into a detailed exploration of this beautiful technique, but suffice to say that through determined and consistent effort, our whole world changes as we begin to experience reality, directly.

With practice of course, we take these particular skills of non-attached awareness into the everyday world, but to begin we need to spend time in quiet meditation.

*For a complete structured home study course of Insight & Loving Kindness Meditation see, Opening the Spiritual Heart, by Michael Kewley. Published by Panna Dipa books.

Through prolonged practice of this beautiful technique, we can begin to establish some wisdom into our real nature as we perhaps for the first time, confront the three characteristics that govern all mental and physical processes. The three characteristics are:

Impermanence (Anicca)
When we slow everything down through the practice of meditation, and cease simply reacting to everything that presents itself to us, we begin to notice this quality of endless change. Nothing stops, not even for a single moment, and the whole of existence including ourselves, is only a never-ending series of changes from a beginningless beginning to an endless end, and nothing is excluded from this process. We ourselves are simply more of the same process, beginning and ending, but never stopping. This includes all mental and physical states.

No-Self (Anatta)
The second characteristic is that of emptiness or No-Self. As we begin to recognize ourselves as a series of never ending processes, we realize that nowhere within these processes is there anything that is separate from them, and so can be called a soul or enduring self. This truth can be experienced by anyone who will earnestly cultivate a sincere Insight Meditation practice and allow the mind to be awakened to the reality that is revealed.

The teaching of No-Soul or enduring Self, is not a belief, it is a truth that has to be realized and fully comprehended by each one of us individually.
To say, I believe in No-Self is foolish and is not how the Dhamma was taught by the Buddha. The teaching of

No-Self is deep and profound and is what actually sets Buddhism apart from other religions. It is unique to Buddhism and was the second great teaching given by the Buddha to his five disciples at the deer park at Sarnath after the Four Noble Truths. In the Pali scriptures it is called the Anattanalakhana Sutta, the marks of No-Self.

Suffering (Dukkha)

When we begin to experience the truth of the first two characteristics, that of non-stopping change and within a process of change, nothing we can call me, mine, self or soul, we can at last understand the nature of Dukkha. There is no thought, no feeling, no emotion and no bodily or mental sensation that can be called mine, that I am the owner of, or that I ultimately control, and so consequently, any attachment to any of these things leads only to unhappiness, suffering and the experience of unsatisfactoryness.

Eradicating the experience of Dukkha from our lives is the purpose of the teachings of the Buddha, and the direct path to that goal is the practice of Insight Meditation. This is the technique whereby each one of us can realise our true nature, beyond belief and blind faith, and so free ourselves from the bonds of delusion that so powerfully bind us to the wheel of suffering.

Insight Meditation, as part of a religious package is found only in Buddhism, but can be cultivated by anyone, Buddhist or not. Insight Meditation therefore transcends all religion and has the function only of revealing the truth to us. It has sometimes been described as being cold and impersonal because through the technique we experience the mind and body without opinion or judgement, and so, almost as if to balance that, we are to cultivate the third part of our daily meditation programme that of loving kindness.

Loving Kindness
Metta Bhavana

For human beings there are many kinds of love we can experience. Love for our families, our friends and even our possessions. In fact, we can use the expression 'I love', towards almost anything. However, what we are really saying is, 'I like'.

This liking, so often confused for love, is really only attachment. We love our family, simply because they are ours, and not for any special qualities they may possess, we love our children for the same reason. We love our friends, our pets, our cars, our houses. We love our towns and even our countries in exactly the same way, attachment.

This attachment is established in our delusive concept of 'self', and so when these things no longer please or satisfy us, for whatever reason, our love for them changes to anger, disappointment and even hatred. This cannot be called real love, or spiritual love, for being based in attachment to 'self', it does not, and cannot, have any enduring qualities. As we look around the world we see greed and hatred, manifesting in quarrels, disputes, argument, divorce, and even wars, as people seem unable to live with the things they once thought that they loved. The development of Spiritual Love or Loving Kindness, is considered to be very important by Buddhists and is the cornerstone of that well-known Buddhist quality, tolerance. The meditation on Loving Kindness is a very powerful technique and as with all Buddhist meditation techniques should never be regarded as an ineffectual practice whereby we try to like everyone and everything in the world, even the things we really hate.

Rather it should be understood as the natural enhancement to Insight Meditation by opening the heart with patience, love and acceptance to the world and its ways.

It is not possible to like everyone and everything in life, for there will always be things that we are attracted towards and things we are repelled by. This is natural, but as the practice Loving Kindness unfolds we find that we are more and more able to live in harmony with all the pleasant and unpleasant things that we encounter. We no longer waste our time making judgements and formulating opinions about people and events and we are able to accept them as they are. We begin to understand that we all make mistakes and that as humans, we are all suffering to a greater or lesser extent. The law of Kamma operates whether we realise it or not, and there is no need for us to add our comments to events and situations when the results of any action, wholesome or not, cannot be separated from the original state of mind. No-one gets away with anything and we all have to pay the price for what we do. Violence and horror in the world stem from ignorance. Wise beings always act with love and compassion. Therefore we should try to be wise in our dealings with others and develop a heart that is worthy of the wisest of beings.

It is very easy in life to love the things we like, such as puppies and kittens our children and the people we want to marry. But all conditions change and on a cold and wintry night when the once cuddly puppy is now a large and demanding dog needing to be taken for his evening walk, we may not feel so loving towards it.

With the development of Loving Kindness we recognise that all beings are as they are, good or bad, and if we spend our whole time trying to change them so that they are perfect for us, we only make them suffer as well as ourselves. When we can understand this, we can learn to 'let go'. Not out of contempt because they do not please us, but rather from love and acceptance.

Buddhist Loving Kindness is a love that gives and yet asks for nothing in return. It is not part of the barter system of life, '*I will love you but you must love me back*', and so is unconditional. It is boundless because it touches all beings equally and without exception. In the moment when there is Loving Kindness for one being, there is spontaneously, Loving Kindness for all beings. It cannot be any other way. Loving Kindness is always universal. According to the Buddhist scriptures. There are many benefits for the practitioner of Loving Kindness and these are listed as follows:

One always sleeps peacefully.
One suffers no evil dreams.
One becomes dear to all beings.
One is protected by deities.
One cannot be hurt by poisons.
Concentration comes easily.
Ones features become serene.
One dies on confused.
If complete enlightenment is not attained within this lifetime, one is born into the highest of the heaven realms.

Loving kindness is the developing and giving of true love. Love that has no boundaries or conditions. Love that is blameless and faultless. Love that is all-encompassing.

This technique of meditation should end the lay Buddhist daily meditation 'sit', which began with Mindfulness of Breathing and was followed by Insight Meditation.

This practice is enough for enlightenment, according to the Buddha, nothing more is needed. The development of concentration, awareness and love will take us to the furthest shore. However, we should always attempt to take our understanding, gained through our formal meditation, into everyday activity. Meditation is not used to escape the pressures of the world, but to reveal to ourselves exactly where these pressures really begin and end.

So here in brief is an outline of the lay Buddhists daily meditation practice something to be performed once or twice a day, depending upon commitment and circumstance, with the purpose of developing a calm and peaceful heart, a wise and loving heart, and a heart that is not easily shaken by the vicissitudes of life.

Reverence

At one time there were two hermits living together in seclusion and practicing religious austerities. At the end of forty eight years one hermit left the other to get married and enjoy family life. Soon to him and his wife a son was born, and the former hermit and his wife took the baby to the remaining hermit to ask for his blessing. To the parents the hermit said, 'May you live long.' To the child he said nothing. When the parents asked him why he had not blessed the child he told them that the baby would only live for seven more days, and he did not know how to prevent its death. He advised the parents to seek out the Buddha who may be able to help them to save the life of the child.

The parents soon found the Buddha and asked for his blessing. To them, he said 'May you live long.' To the child he said nothing.

When the parents asked about the child the Buddha told them the same as the hermit. But in this instance, he knew of a way to prevent the death. The Buddha told the former hermit and his wife to build a Pavilion at the entrance of their house and to lay the child on a couch within the Pavilion. When this was done, the Buddha sent monks to chant special stanzas for the baby to prevent harm befalling it. On the seventh day, the Buddha himself attended the chanting.

Unseen by human eyes many devas from the heaven realms, attracted by the sound of the Buddhist disciples chanting the stanzas, arrived at the Pavilion, as well as a fierce ogre who had come to take away the life of the baby. However, as more powerful devas arrived, the ogre was forced to step further and further away from the entrance until he was eventually unable to carry out his task.

The chanting continued through the night until finally the

child was taken up from the couch and brought before the Buddha. This time the Buddha blessed the child and said, 'May you live long.'

Many years later, when the child had grown he visited the Jetavana monastery. The monks residing there realised immediately who he was and asked the Buddha this question. "For ordinary beings is there a way of gaining longevity?"

The Buddha replied, "By respecting and honouring the wise and virtuous, one not only gains longevity, but also beauty, happiness and strength."

The Buddha then spoke in verse as follows:

> For one who always respects those
> who are wiser and more virtuous,
> four benefits can be expected,
> longevity, beauty, happiness and strength.

Dhammapada: verse 109

It seems that now, with only a few exceptions, reverence in the Western world is a thing of the past. A reverential attitude towards those people and institutions traditionally held in high regard is no longer cultivated or even expected by society at large, and even if it was, there seems to be so few opportunities for its practice, as to make its development pointless.

The church, possibly the most obvious focus for reverence, can no more be held by many in the same high esteem, as it struggles within its own confusion regarding social and moral issues, being at times greatly divided and thus presenting no firm foundation for the confidence of its supporters.

Politicians and world leaders are found out time and time again to be dishonest and corrupt whilst royalty in the majority of countries where it still survives, plays only a figurehead role with no real power at its disposal. To what then can ordinary people in the West direct their attention with a sense of respect and humility?

From the Buddhist perspective, the East still holds many opportunities to develop and offer respect, and now growing slowly but steadily the same opportunities present themselves in the West. The familiar sight in the East of quiet humble figure wearing a simple orange robe that denotes the Buddhist monk walking silently, with eyes downcast through the streets of the village or a major town in Burma, Sri Lanka or Thailand, is for many the perfect opportunity for making merit by paying respect and offering alms.

This is because the shaven head, the orange robe and the attitude of complete humility are outward signs of a tradition, whose upholders, namely the monastic community, dedicate themselves to a life of moral purity and spiritual advancement through meditation and study. They also work for social causes, to help those in difficult circumstances, although in a strictly non political way. For the Buddhist, whether lay or monastic, the development of a reverential attitude is very important. Reverence stems from humility and humility only becomes well-established through the erosion of our wrong view or misunderstanding of self. Pride and arrogance are manifestations of a mind still very much caught up in its own importance, always believing its views and opinions to be the best. The continuing attachment to these mental formations leads only to a stronger, more powerful ego and consequently, a more closed mind. If you already believe you have all the answers, to whom do you need to listen?

As practicing lay Buddhists we naturally develop the feelings of reverence towards the Buddha, whom we can consider as the physical manifestation of wisdom. Not a god. Not a magical being. But someone who through his own supreme effort, attained the ultimate goal of enlightenment perfect wisdom.

Enhancing this feeling of reverence comes gratitude for not only did he attain the ultimate goal, he travelled and taught for the remainder of his life, ensuring that we too almost two thousand six hundred years later, can benefit from his experience of Nibbana.

We can also extend our feelings of reverence towards the actual teachings of the Buddha.

So often this has been translated so that it sounds dry and uninspiring, however with the verses in the Dhammapada it is sure that this is not to be the way it was intended.

The Buddha spoke in the common language of the people using words and terms they could easily understand. As always, the most profound teachings can always be transmitted simply, retaining their beauty and depth. As ones understanding of the Buddhist teachings deepens an attitude of reverence and respect for their perfect wisdom naturally develops.

Finally, as lay Buddhists we offer our reverence to the community of monks and nuns living the holy life under the Buddha's instruction. Today as in the Buddha's time, the principles are the same. Some minor rules governing conduct may have changed due to circumstance, but the code of moral purity remains the same. Any man or woman from whatever religious or social background, earnestly living a life of simplicity and honesty is worthy of our deepest reverence and respect.

Service

At one time there was a Brahmin who noticed a group of monks arranging their robes as they prepared to enter the city for alms. Whilst he was looking he noticed that some of the monks robes touched the ground and became wet as they brushed the dew on the grass. Immediately he cleared that patch of ground.

The next day, when observing the monks again, he noticed their robes were becoming dirty as they touched the soil in the place where he had cleared the grass the day before. Immediately he covered the bare earth with sand.

In time, he noticed that the monks would perspire in the hot sun, and became soaked when it rained, so he built a rest house for them at the place where they gathered before entering the city on the alms round. When the building was finished, the Brahmin invited the Buddha and his monks for food, and during the gathering explained to the Buddha how the building had come about.

To him the Buddha replied, "Oh Brahmin, the wise perform acts of merit little by little, and gradually and constantly they remove the impurities of moral defilements."

The Buddha then spoke in verse as follows:

By degrees, little by little from moment to moment,
a wise man removed all his impurities,
as a smith removes the dross
of gold or silver.

Dhammapada: verse 239

To the practicing lay Buddhist the notion of service is a very important one and is recognised as the natural extension of wholesome qualities such as generosity and compassion.

Each one of us is a member of a number of societies, varying from the small and intimate family group to the immense and often wholly impersonal national community. However as Buddhists we should be aware of the different groups and communities we are part of and seek ways to contribute to the continuing welfare of our fellow beings.

Both the family group and society as a whole, support and nourish us, and to take without supplying anything in return simply constitutes greed, no matter how subtle it may be.

Naturally, if we consider ourselves as practicing Buddhists, we are already upholding the five precepts, which constitute Right Action.

By living a life based in these five training rules we are already performing a great service to society as we no longer simply act from greed, hatred and delusion, those three fires that burn within us all, but control our actions through gentle restraint. By observing our natural tendencies towards our own selfish desires we are in a position of authority over our own mind. From this position we can review the situation and respond with appropriate action. It is said that '*the mind can be our best friend or our greatest enemy*', but with moral restraint and the practice of awareness we can ensure that the former is the case.

With this training we already contribute greatly to the benefit of all we come into contact with as we no longer blindly support the selfish confusion that already abounds in the world.

As seen earlier, our employment should preferably be one that serves our fellow beings, however, this cannot be the situation for everyone.

The number of people who can be doctors, nurses and health and social workers is small, whilst the factories and offices are packed to capacity by people seeking only a living wage. For these ordinary people the opportunities to serve fellow beings may seem remote, but from the Buddhist perspective they arise endlessly, and we need only to be aware to take advantage of them.

To make oneself available is the key to giving service. After all, the greatest thing we can offer to help anyone is our time and interest. So, whether we simply assist granny with her shopping or housework, or become a prison or hospital visitor, we should always be ready to help and give service.

The Buddha himself was very clear about this:

> One should make haste in performing good deeds.
> One should restrain ones' mind from evil,
> for the mind of one who is slow in doing good,
> tends to delight in doing evil.

Dhammapada: verse 116

Most people who work in society for the benefit of their fellow beings do so quietly and without great reward, seeking only to be of service. Many are ordinary folk with no resources to assist them, however, they give of their time and effort simply because of their good heart. This is most certainly the Buddhist ideal, and although it is not for everyone to work at the deepest levels within society, there are many opportunities daily for all of us to be of service to others. We only need to be aware and be prepared to give of ourselves.

Transference of Merit

At one time there lived in Sarnath a lay follower of the Buddha, who was very fond of giving in charity. His name was Dhammaka. Dhammaka generously offered food and other requisites to the monks and was in fact the leader of a great number of lay supporters in that town. Now Dhammaka was also the father of seven sons and seven daughters, and each one like their father, was virtuous and devoted to giving in charity.

At a time when Dhammaka was very ill and close to death, he made the request that monks should come to him and recite the suttas by his bedside. This they happily did, but as they were reciting the Mahasatipatthana Sutta, the teaching of the Four Foundations of Mindfulness, six decorated chariots from six celestial realms visited Dhammaka with invitations for him to accompany any one of them to their respective worlds.

Dhammaka told them to wait for a while for fear of interrupting the recitation of the sutta. However, the monks thinking they were asked to stop, ended in the recitation and left the house.

A little while later Dhammaka told his children of the six celestial chariots waiting for him, and there and then made his choice to go to the Tusita world and asked his children to throw a garland on the chariot of his choice. He then quietly passed away.

So it is said that the virtuous man rejoices in this world as well as the next.

Here he rejoices, hereafter he rejoices.
One who has performed virtuous deeds
rejoices in both existences.
He rejoices and rejoices greatly
when he sees the purity of his own deeds.

Dhammapada: verse 16

For the most part, merit is a very misunderstood term in the West, primarily because it is not really a part of our religious background. However, even in the East where the making of merit is an integral part of spiritual life, there is little true comprehension as to what merit actually is.

The most common understanding of the 'making of merit', is that by performing an act of generosity towards a needy recipient, especially of a follower of a spiritual path, the value of that good deed will be stored up somewhere to be reclaimed at a later date. Possibly being put towards continuing good fortune in this life, or a good rebirth in the next. It translates as a kind of continuous credit system.

However, there is a negative side to this cosmic bank balance brought into effect when one displays too many tendencies of greed, selfishness or cruelty, leaving ones' account overdrawn. This condition can only be remedied by deliberately making penances or performing acts of charity until the spiritual bank balance is back in credit.

According to Buddhist thought, this is not the correct understanding of merit. Merit, it must be understood is not the result of any action, but of the actual mental state experienced in determining the action in any given moment. To give for example, when the mind is filled only with feelings of generosity and love, produces great merit and is of benefit to both the giver and the receiver alike. The same action however, performed when the mind is filled with feelings of resentment or hostility and regret, and seen only from the advantage of personal self aggrandisement, brings only benefit to the recipient and little, if any, to the giver. Without pure intention it is sometimes better not to give at all.

This story from the Dhammapada illustrates this very clearly.

At one time, King Pasenadi of Kosala came to pay homage to the Buddha.

Whilst talking, the king revealed that before setting out on his journey he had been called to confiscate all the possessions of a miserly man, who had died early in the day and left no heir. This man, although very wealthy had never given anything in charity and was indeed reluctant to spend his money, even on himself. He ate only sparingly and wore only the cheapest and most coarse of clothes. On hearing this, the Buddha told the king about this man in a past existence. At this time he was also a very wealthy person.

At one time, a fully enlightened being came and stood at the door of his house and asked for alms. The man seeing him, told his wife to prepare some food and to make an offering. The wife thought that this was such a rare act for her husband to offer anything to anyone, that she would fill the alms bowl to the brim So that he would have sufficient to eat that day. Later as the man was returning from a business meeting in the town he passed the enlightened being and noticed that his alms bowl was filled to capacity. Seeing that his wife had offered so much he began to harbour such thoughts as, 'Oh what a waste of good food. This one will only sleep the day away now. It would have been better to give the food to my servants, at least they would have given me better service.' Because of this way of thinking, of regretting a wholesome action, the rich man was born again into wealth in this lifetime, but without any disposition to spend it, even on himself.

The Buddha then spoke in verse as follows:

> Wealth destroys the foolish,
> but it cannot destroy those seeking Nibbana.
> By his craving for wealth,
> the fool destroys himself
> as he would destroy others.

Dhammapada: verse 335

To give with a glad heart and without regret is the mark of true generosity, and such acts are always meritorious.

In English, we use the expression 'kindness is its own reward', and this is also the Buddhist understanding. The reward of kindness is the mental state produced by that very kindness, and the more we experience wholesome mental states the further along the spiritual path we go. The teaching of the Buddha is the way to eradicate all unwholesome and ultimately harmful states of mind. This practice is also known as the Vishudhimagga, *The path of Purification*.

By using the meditation techniques taught by the Buddha we more and more often, 'let go', of the mental states that have their roots in greed, hatred and delusion, and discover that the very act of 'letting go', helps manifest the wholesome aspects of mind, such as generosity love and wisdom. As practicing meditators we realise that mind fore runs all conditions, so we begin to understand that it is the quality of the mental states that determines the quality of the action. Any action preceding from a mind no longer dominated by the notion of 'self', with the objective of gain and reward, will naturally experience the greatest reward of all, that of continuing development along the spiritual path. Actually, we cannot even say that this is a reward at all. This is the natural consequence of applying the teachings of the Buddha to our lives.

Perhaps we can now see that the ardent Buddhist, striving in his or her practice of Dhamma, performs meritorious actions more and more often, as his or her mind becomes more pure. The attachment to 'self', is lessened and purity of actions and speech becomes the natural way to respond to the world. On occasion, this way of being can lead to some embarrassment when pointed out by others, but when wholesome actions become a natural way of life, why even mention them?

However, this is not the end of the story.

Anyone who has ever attended Buddhist meditation retreats will remember that the final meditation performed by the group as a whole, is the meditation on the Transference of Merit.

To spend any length of time in meditation, whether hours, days or weeks brings with it a great merit. To hear the Dhamma taught whilst undergoing such discipline is also meritorious and so at the end of the meditation retreat our mind may have experienced some fundamental change to the feelings encountered, and possibly the wisdom gained. It is at this point, we make the most profound gesture.

Any merit we may have accrued through our long hours of practice we offer to share with all beings. The mental state we deliberately cultivate at the end of what may have been weeks of difficult meditation practice is that of Metta, Loving Kindness.

As we sit quietly with our minds at peace we offer all beings without exception, any merit we have gained, thus at least mentally, sharing that which we have worked so hard for.

This is experienced as a great joy, and one feels privileged to be in such a position. This is how merit manifests.

In the East the Transference of Merit is generally directed towards ones dearly departed friends and relatives, that they may be happy in their new rebirth. Although this is not part of Western culture, it is not difficult to see the benefits of such practice. Having performed a meritorious deed, such as offering alms food to monks one goes to the grave of a friend or relative and offers the merit to them, so that they may be well and happy, wherever they have taken birth. As always, it is the mental attitude we are concerned with and the mind that gives and then offers the result of that giving to others contains a degree of purity outside our usual way of being in the world. Such a mind by its very nature, is already developing further merit.

Merit is difficult to understand. As long as we hold the view that it is the reward for something, we will be confused. It may be said that it is better to 'let go', of the whole notion of making merit and live each moment in the present, cultivating the mind that naturally wants to help and be of service, allowing the outcome to take care of itself.

Rejoicing in the Merit of Others

At one time the Buddha was on alms round in Savatthi when he came across a number of youths beating a snake with sticks. When questioned, the youths said that they were beating the snake because they were afraid it may bite them.

To them the Buddha replied, "If you do not want to be harmed you should not harm others. If you harm others, you will not find happiness in your next life."

Then the Buddha spoke in verse as follows:

> He who seeks his own happiness
> by oppressing others who also seek happiness,
> will not find happiness in their next life.

> He who seeks his own happiness
> by not oppressing others who also seek happiness,
> will find happiness in the next life.

Dhammapada: verses 131 & 132

The world is made up of unenlightened beings. Beings who have not experienced the truth of reality, and consequently cannot see clearly as to the way of things. These beings relate to the world through their continuing action and reaction, taking everything experienced through the mind and the senses to be real and have lasting value. They have not penetrated the truths of change, no-self, and suffering.

Without developing wisdom through reflection and meditation, the truth of reality cannot be known, and as a result of this inherent ignorance, suffering occurs as we perpetually interpret the world through our delusion of 'self'.

Now, ignorance is not a crime, it is not a sin, but it is a blindness, and it is our purpose as Buddhists to learn to see clearly and to bring a light into the darkness that is ignorance.

Happily, within the mass of struggling humanity, there are some beings who are ardent and devoted to the way that leads to the direct realisation of the truth. It is to these few fellow men and women that ordinary people offer their respect.

When one is fortunate enough to meet and spend time with a being well established on the path, not necessarily a Buddhist monk or nun, it is a truly joyful experience. By observing first hand, the humility and simplicity of such beings, one can recognise the unfolding of the way that leads to the end of suffering, and this can inspire us to follow their example.

Wisdom in another is a wonderful thing to see and it is very easy to recognise the merit thus accrued and rejoice in it. With a happy heart, we can all share in the efforts made by an individual attempting to put into practice the teachings of the Buddha and know that because of these efforts we too can move nearer the goal. What is possible for one is possible for all.

Each day as lay Buddhists we offer our respects to the Sangha, the community of men and women, monks and nuns from the past and present, who have attained through their own ceaseless efforts the goal of the practice and have thereby been freed from the bonds of suffering. These beings are worthy of our deepest respect and admiration and to celebrate in their endeavour is a natural response to anyone also walking the path to self purification.

However, in ordinary life there are also many beings we can offer our respect towards. People who work tirelessly for the benefit of others so that their suffering, whether worldly or not, may be less. People working in third world countries, mostly unsung, whose great efforts help many, perhaps thousands of poor people trapped in their environment. Men and women working within our own country helping to find homes for the homeless and food for the hungry. People working with abused children and the basic rights of all beings including animals. These people, who work for the welfare of others, not only create happier conditions for the people they help, but in their very attitude of caring their demonstration of love and compassion make for themselves much merit.

This merit, we can all share and celebrate in, and can truly be seen as a light in the world.

Hearing the Dhamma

At one time there were thirty youths enjoying themselves on a picnic in the forest just outside their home town. Each youth had brought his wife, except one who was accompanied by a prostitute. As the day wore on it was noticed that the prostitute, as well as many valuable items belonging to the party, had gone missing, and so the whole assembly set out to find the thief and bring her back.

While searching however, they came across the Buddha sitting under a tree. The party respectfully asked the Buddha, if he had seen anyone go past that way, but instead of answering their question, he gave a short discourse. So impressed were the young men that they immediately asked for admission into the order of monks.

At the Jetavana monastery, they practised earnestly, and upon hearing a particular discourse from the Buddha one night, all became completely enlightened.

When other monks commented upon this the Buddha replied in verse as follows:

> An intelligent man,
> even though he is associated with the wise man
> only from moment,
> quickly understands the Dhamma,
> just as the tongue knows a taste of soup.

Dhammapada: verse 65

After the Buddha had attained his perfect enlightenment at the foot of the Bodhi Tree, in what is now, Budh Gaya, he was faced with a difficult problem. His attainment was so profound yet so subtle, that he felt it would be realisable to only a few even with his expert guidance. The two people who would have been able to grasp it had both died. They were Alarma the Kalama and Udaka Ramaputta, his former teachers. With their years of devoted practice to their own particular meditation styles, it would not have been difficult to turn them towards the way of realisation.

The Buddha even considered not teaching at all. To be pounded by questions from all sides, some sincere, some not, some designed only to further an argument, would be tiring indeed, and perhaps it would be better to avoid that situation entirely. However, it was now that a great compassion arose in the Buddha. With his divine eye he saw the suffering beings in the world and realised that he had to share what he had discovered. The scriptures describe this beautiful moment with the words *'for the sake of those beings with only a little dust in the eyes'*.

Having made this important decision, he set out to meet his five former colleagues at the deer park in Sarnath, where he would begin to teach the Four Noble Truths and the Eightfold Path, and begin to establish the Dhamma in the world.

Now, almost two thousand six hundred years later this Dhamma is still being taught, truly and perfectly preserved by the community of Buddhist monks and nuns in its traditional form and language.

In modern times it is not necessary for anyone to travel outside of their own country in order to hear the Buddhist teaching. Many thousands of books have been written, and the very best teachers from all traditions freely travel from one place to another in order to share the Dhamma.

To sit at the feet of such a being, imbued with wisdom and living the life of the Dhamma practitioner and to hear him or her speak of the way to incorporate the Buddhist teachings into our everyday life, is always an inspiring and a joyful occasion. Naturally, the style of teaching will differ from person to person and from tradition to tradition, but in all cases, the transmission will be a heartfelt attitude of sharing something that will without doubt, benefit the lives of any who put these words into practice.

The two main approaches to Dhamma teaching are based on the scriptures and tradition, as it has been handed down since the first Great Council of Arahats three months after the death of the Buddha, and by direct experience of living a life according to its tenets.

Of course, both approaches are correct and often mixed to demonstrate that the teaching is a timeless one and that scripture and tradition have not become outdated, since the problems that faced the people in India during the time of the Buddha have exactly the same root causes as those facing us in the modern world. Those causes are greed, hatred and delusion, the three ever burning and all consuming fires within us. As lay Buddhists we have two clear duties. The first is to develop a meditation practice, that will open our mind to the way of things, and the second to read and study the scriptures so that we are able to understand the words of the Buddha.

One without the other is an imbalance. We could read all the books and scriptures there are in the world, and still not know what the Buddha taught.

The whole teaching came from his meditation, and to understand properly we have to return to that very meditation. Buddhist practice is not about thinking of Dhamma. It is of living Dhamma, each to the best of their ability. Reading and studying alone will not change our life. We must cultivate clear comprehension into the Buddha's way, by applying his teaching moment after moment.

To hear the Dhamma means to listen to the teachings of the Buddha with a heart and mind that is open. We must be ready to change our usual way of thinking and behaving, and be prepared to put into practice a way of life that will not only benefit ourselves, but ultimately all beings.

When the Buddha described the Dhamma he said it was, *'that which is good in the beginning, good in the middle, and good in the end'*. In other words, perfect and without flaw.

Now in the West there is no shortage of books, audio and video cassettes, all easily available for the student of Buddhism to rent or buy. However, as good as these things are they are always secondary to the benefit received from the personal instruction given by a teacher of good reputation. It has become the tradition, especially in Theravada Buddhism that the monks and nuns live in a close relationship with the laity, and it must be considered very important that any aspiring Buddhist take advantage of this opportunity for contact.

There are many Buddhist centres of all traditions throughout the United Kingdom and Europe. No one will ever be turned away and the Dhamma will always be offered.

Teaching the Dhamma

At one time there was a very eloquent teacher of Dhamma, called Upananda. He would preach to others not to be greedy, to have only a few wants, to live simply and practice the monks austerities. However, he did not practise what he preached and took for himself many offerings that were made by lay people without sharing them with the rest of the monastic community.

On one occasion Upananda was invited to spend the three months rainy season at a small village monastery by two young monks who had heard him preach and had been impressed by his eloquence. He asked first of all, how many robes each monk received at the end of the rains retreat, and when it was revealed that each monk only received one robe, he decided not to stay, but instead he left a pair of slippers at the monastery and moved on.

At another monastery he learned that each monk received two robes at the end of the rains retreat, and there he left his staff. Further along he discovered a monastery where each monk received three robes, and there he left his water bottle. Finally he came to a monastery where each monk received four robes at the end of the rains retreat, and there he decided to stay.

At the end of the three months he returned to the other monasteries where he had left some of his personal belongings and claimed his share of the robes. He collected everything up in a cart and set off towards his own monastery.

On his way home, he was asked to intercede in an argument between two young monks over the sharing of robes and a valuable velvet blanket. Upananda shared the robes equally between them but kept the blanket for himself for having acted as arbitrator. The two young monks were not happy

with this decision and so reported the matter to the Buddha. To them, the Buddha said, "One who teaches others should first teach himself, and then act as he has taught."
The Buddha then spoke in verse as follows:

One should first establish oneself in what is proper,
only then should one teach others.
A wise man should not incur reproach.

Dhammapada: verse 158

It must be obvious to all that before we can lead others along the path we must first be thoroughly familiar with that path ourselves. As lay Buddhists it is our responsibility to become quite certain of the Buddhist teachings before we presume to impart it to others.
This does not mean that we have to read, study, memorise each sutta, verse and saying of the Buddha. Rather, we should understand the spirit of the teaching as opposed to remembering the academic letter of it. We have to investigate the Buddhas' words and understand from our own experience, the truth of them. Our attention should be directed towards deepening our understanding of morality and meditation, and not only understanding them but to make them part and parcel of our everyday life. The teaching of the Buddha is about the practice of perfecting ourselves.
It is the business of doing, not thinking about or telling others how they should be.
Another story from the Dhammapada may help to illustrate this important point.

At one time, Thera Padanikatissa was put in charge of a large number of junior monks, all of whom had received a meditation subject from the Buddha. He led them into the forest to begin their meditation practice.

Thera Padanikatissa would always exhort the young monks to be ever mindful and diligent in their practice, whilst he unknown to them would sneak away to a quiet spot and sleep. Late into the night when the monks were ready to go to bed Thera Padanikatissa would wake up and tell them all to go back to their practice. This would happen two or three times each night until the monks were completely exhausted and could not summon any concentration for meditation or even the recitation of the texts.

Eventually they decided to see if their teacher really was as zealous and diligent as he claimed to be, and so they followed him one day and caught him sleeping. At this discovery the monks cried, "We are ruined. Our teacher knows only how to scold us while he himself is just wasting his time sleeping. Our teacher does not practise what he preaches." With this complaint they went to see the Buddha. The Buddha listened to them and replied "Monks, one who wants to teach others must first teach himself and then conduct himself properly."

Then the Buddha spoke in verse as follows:

> One should act as one teaches others.
> Only with oneself thoroughly tamed
> should one tame others.
> To tame oneself is difficult indeed.

Dhammapada: verse 159

Teaching others is a great responsibility and having established confidence in our understanding of practice our approach to sharing it with others must be appropriate. For those truly wishing to hear the word of the Buddha a suitable time and place will not be an excessive demand, whilst those who are merely curious or wish to promote their own views and opinions at the expense of Dhamma, *'right here, right now'*, seems to be the only consideration.

If we reflect upon the words of the Mangala Sutta, the Buddhist teaching as to what constitutes a blessing in life, we will encounter, the expression, *'timely hearing of the Dhamma'*, which simply put, means that time and place have a great bearing on the teaching, if it is to have any value at all. In general conversation across a workbench in a factory or in a busy canteen at lunchtime the words of Dhamma are lost in others personal points of view, while the overall environment of spiritual darkness is present.

For those people whose interest is deeper than idle curiosity being patient and waiting for the right circumstances will not deter them. In fact, making some effort to hear the Dhamma will actually assist in their valuing of it.

The Buddhist teaching is not only relevant to the world of today, but also supremely practical in all situations. However, this can be better understood in more appropriate surroundings, such as a shrine room or a quiet group sitting

What we teach is important and should not be coloured by our own interpretations. The Buddhist teaching, as collected and preserved in the Tipitika, the three baskets of the cannon, also called the Pali Canon, can be seen as dry and academic, but it is to this that many monks and scholars devote their lives, developing a clear intellectual understanding of the subtleties of Dhamma.

Other monks and nuns spend their time in meditation and reflection upon the heart of the Buddha Dhamma. This heart, the same for all traditions of Buddhism is nothing more than the Four Noble Truths. The truth of suffering or unsatisfactoryness, the truth of its cause, the truth of its cessation and the truth of the way that leads to its cessation. This is the first teaching in Buddhism, but it is also the last. True realisation, Nibbana, lies only in the penetration of these Four Noble Truths.

If we are in a position to teach others our echo of Dhamma must be clear and reflected through our heart, thought, word and deed, for we must all fundamentally teach by example and not like Thera Padanikatissa. As Buddhists we are not to knock on people's doors or to stop them in the street in the hope of persuading them to accept Buddhism as their new religion. Buddhism is not and never has been, a religion of conversion, and to behave in this manner would be considered as offensive, for each one of us has the right to choose their own spiritual path.

However, we can open up our meetings to guests and quietly without any pressure, inform them of the Buddha's way. This is most certainly in keeping with the Buddhist compassion for those beings, '*with just a little dust in the eyes*', and even if these people leave, never to return, we have provided them with the opportunity to hear the Dhamma in the right way. After that it is for them to choose.

Teaching the Dhamma is important, but our feeling must be one of sharing something special and not bullying someone into our way of thinking. Of course, the basis of teaching must be to practice what we preach, so the concept of sharing Dhamma, so *that others may benefit* may be more useful than the idea of teaching something that will *do them good*. In matters of teaching, humility is always the watchword.

Correcting the Wrong Views of Others

At one time, the monks Assaji and Punabbasaka, with their five hundred disciples were residing at Kitagiri village. Whilst staying there, they made their living by planting flowering plants and fruit trees for their own personal gain, thus breaking the fundamental precepts of monks.

When the Buddha heard about this practice, he sent his two chief disciples, venerable Sariputta, and the venerable Mahamogallana to stop them from committing further misconduct, saying, "Tell the monks not to destroy the faith, confidence and generosity of the lay supporters by these acts of misconduct. If any monk disobeys he must be made to leave the monastery. Do not hesitate to do as I have told you, for only a fool dislikes being given good advice and being forbidden to perform wrongdoings."

The Buddha then spoke in verse as follows:

> The man of wisdom should admonish others.
> He should give advice and prevent others from doing wrong.
> Such a man is held dear by the gods
> and disliked only by the foolish.

Dhammapada: verse 77

'Before you can teach Dhamma you must know Dhamma'

The Buddha

One of the results of a committed meditation practice is an increased understanding into the law of Kamma, the universal process of cause and effect. We begin to see more clearly that everything we think, say and do, has an effect upon ourselves, others and the world around us. Armed with this knowledge we speak and behave in a manner less likely to have harmful results and we become increasingly aware of our on-going mental states as something we can experience, but is not what we are. Not an ultimate reality that has to be acted upon, but only a series of habits and conditionings, arising from a *beginningless beginning* and moving on to an *endless end*. As we see our fears, hopes dreams, emotions and selfish desires as visions displayed on an empty screen, in reality not touching us at all, our life becomes quieter, more peaceful and harmonious and less prone to simple action and reaction. However, as we recognise Kammic Law more and more, we also understand that, '*as it is for me, so it is for all beings*', and it is this very awareness that leads to a dilemma.

When we see others performing actions that by their very nature can only produce harmful results as a consequence, do we stay in the background and remain silent, or do we step in and give advice that if acted upon, would be beneficial?

People in the world hold many kinds of wrong views which themselves are born of ignorance of not knowing the truth of reality. Until we can begin to break through the net of ignorance that prevents us from attaining perfect spiritual liberation, every step we take in the world will begin with the wrong foot. The teaching of the Buddha, if practiced and applied will naturally lead us to a place where we will experience the truth of reality for ourselves as it manifests moment after moment, therefore making the holding of views and opinions redundant. We can be free from the power of ignorance if we apply ourselves to the task in hand, and once we have begun we are in a position to be of service to others.

As Buddhists, we recognise with compassion, the suffering caused by ignorance of all the many beings that live in the world. To these beings, *without exception*, we offer our Loving Kindness with the wish that they may be well and happy. However, we also recognise that if we are in a position to assist others avoid suffering through their own delusion, we should act accordingly.

As said earlier, we are not to go out into the streets looking for converts to our way of living, but we should offer our help whenever and wherever it is needed. To attempt to change the way others think and consequently their behaviour, is always to stand on dangerous ground. If any intervention is deemed necessary a definite strategy is required.

We must choose the most appropriate time and place and in the manner of all Buddhist teaching, simply and quietly and most importantly, with humility, offer our help or council and leave it for their consideration.

Here we have to be very careful that we make no claims upon the other person, believing that because they have listened to what we had to say, they may be interested in the whole Buddhist outlook, or if they have simply ignored our advice they are not worth our future efforts. Again, both these attitudes are based in attachment and are not worthy of anyone truly offering assistance to a fellow being. The social and spiritual position of the lay Buddhist is not to press themselves forward, but to be available, to be of service should the need arise. Correcting the wrong views of others can only be accomplished when our own views are correct, and even then, should be seen as a duty if there is an obvious harm apparent in anothers' action. In this instance, it is for us to tactfully illustrate the law of cause and effect as best we can and leave any developing Dhamma strictly up to the individual.

As human beings we all develop at our own pace and because of our inherent potential. For those already established on the path we should remember that if we can help we should help. If we can't help, we shouldn't interfere.
This is the way of Dhamma.

Walking the Path

Part Four

Walking the Path

The Real Path

At one time the venerable Ananda asked the Buddha whether the fundamental instructions to disciples given by preceding Buddhas were the same as those of the Buddha himself.

To him the Buddha replied that the instructions given to disciples, by all Buddhas whether past, present or future are contained in the following verse.

The Buddha then spoke in verse as follows:

> To give up wrong doing,
> to develop righteousness,
> to purify one's own mind.
> These are the teachings of the Buddhas.

Dhammapada: verse 183

It has been said that Buddhism is the fastest growing religion in the West, and although there are as many reasons for people turning towards it as there are people, one of the major factors for this growth must be its relevance to today's modern society.

Naturally, all societies are made up of individuals and these individuals, unless already enlightened are consumed by their desires, cravings and attachments along with their fears, hatred and aversions. These mental formations are bundled together, and held in place by spiritual ignorance, the delusion as to the reality of human existence. So it was in the time of the Buddha almost two thousand six hundred years ago, and so it is now. All beings, whether past, present or future are responsible for their own suffering and discontent and the whole of the Buddhas teaching is directed towards the complete eradication of suffering in our lives by leading us to a place where we can realise the truth of reality for ourselves.

However, to quote from the Dhammapada again.

> You yourselves must make the effort,
> Buddhas only point the way.
> Those who practice tranquillity and insight meditation,
> are freed from the bonds of delusion.

Dhammapada: verse 276

It is clear from this verse that we cannot be carried along the path to liberation by another and that we must take each step for ourselves. There are no gods or deities here to pray to or assist us, only our own determined effort. If this effort is maintained we will, without doubt, arrive at the *Other Shore*. This is the teaching of the Buddha.

A promise of a better life after death is not the way of Buddhism, for the fruits of our practice can be experienced here and now. "Nibbana," said the Buddha, "is realisable in this very lifetime."

It is true to say that the Buddhist way of life is a very practical and realistic way to live in today's modern society. To outsiders it may appear strange that anyone would want to live a life that is so much different from their own. A life that stresses peace and goodwill to all beings, and holds all life dear. Our mental attitudes may also seem strange when we refrain from criticism and placing blame, no matter what the apparent justification. However, to live in peace with all beings is the goal of the Buddhist in society. As we understand the law of Kamma more and more, we see that there is no need for blaming others, for everything we do will surely come back to us.

It may seem that in many instances, the practicing Buddhist is out of step with various aspects of Western culture. By working quietly and without imposition, developing the moral and mental obligations that the Buddha taught, we may even feel this ourselves. However, the Path is not an easy one and only a few are convinced of its value. For ourselves we have to cultivate the qualities of determination and steadfastness, and the knowledge that this way takes us only in one direction, to complete liberation, to the overcoming of sorrow, suffering and the whole realm of human dissatisfaction.

As lay Buddhists we apply ourselves to the basic practice of upholding the Five Precepts and in so doing meet the requirement of *giving up wrong doing.*

When we are able to do this, no matter what desires or aversions may be arising, our behaviour and action will be appropriate. This is to go far beyond personal flights of fancy and put our faith and confidence in something much more worthy. The teachings of an enlightened being.

In order to *develop righteousness*, we have to not only live in a way that causes no harm to ourselves and others but actively be of service to them. This can be achieved, as we have seen, by the cultivation of the Ten Perfections, those qualities brought to perfection by the Buddha in previous lives. To list them again, they are:

GENEROSITY	PATIENCE
MORALITY	HONESTY
RENUNCIATION	RESOLUTION
WISDOM	LOVING KINDNESS
ENERGY	EQUANIMITY

Naturally, to become perfect in any one of these ten qualities would be a huge spiritual achievement let alone bring all ten to that state. But our attitude must be one of patient development of making the most of each opportunity that arises and cultivating the determination to try again each time we fail.

To *purify the mind* is the highest ideal of any aspiring Buddhist. To completely eradicate the smallest trace of greed, hatred and delusion, and in so doing, replace them with the four highest mental states of Loving Kindness, Compassion, Sympathetic Joy and Equanimity, will bring the greatest of benefits to ourselves and all other beings, as we no longer simply contribute to the confusion that already abounds in the world.

Buddhism is not a selfish religion, although it does first demand that we put our own spiritual house in order before we begin to work with others. Buddhism also teaches us to be self-reliant. To blame others for our past, present or future conditions is the mark of an ignorant being. We ourselves are in control of our own lives if only we knew it, and how we think speak and act now will sow the seeds for all our futures.

This final story from the Dhammapada illustrates this point:

At one time there was a lay disciple of the Buddha named Culakala who upheld the eight precepts and spent the whole of the full moon night listening to discourses by monks at the Jetavana monastery. In the early morning as he was washing his face in a pond near the monastery some thieves dropped a bundle of stolen possessions near him.

The owners of the possessions seeing him with a bundle immediately assumed that he was one of the thieves and attacked him and beat him hard. Fortunately some slave girls

who had arrived to fetch water knew of Culakala and vouched that he was not the thief. Because of this Culakala was let off. When the Buddha was told about the incident, he said to Culakala,
"You have been let off not only because the slave girl spoke up for you, but also because in your heart you are not a thief, and therefore innocent. Those who do wrong suffer for it in later lives but those who perform good and honest deeds are reborn in the higher worlds or better, realise Nibbana."
The Buddha then spoke in verse as follows:

By oneself is wrong done, and by oneself is one defiled.
By oneself is good done, and by oneself is one purified.
Purity and impurity depend entirely on oneself.
No one can purify another.

Dhammapada: verse 165

The message of this verse is perfectly clear and takes Buddhism far away from the usual realm of religion. We cannot ask for forgiveness from any superior being, nor can we at death repent our wrongdoings. As Buddhists we take ourselves to be responsible for ourselves, and although we may find we are often under the influence of others ultimately it is ourselves that will reap the consequences of our thoughts, words and actions.
The teaching of all the Buddhas past, present and future is the same,

You yourselves must make the effort,
Buddhas only point the way.

Dhammapada: verse 276

and this lifetime is the perfect opportunity for us to put these teachings into practice.

At the age of 80 in a small village called Kusinara the Buddha finally passed away, leaving us with his last teaching for suffering humanity:

Whatever has the nature to arise
also has the nature to decay.
With mindfulness work diligently
to realise these truths for yourselves.

May all beings be happy

Becoming a Buddhist

It is often asked, "How do I become a Buddhist?"
The answer is simple, by living in accordance with the Buddhist teaching. When one lives in this way, one is already a Buddhist.

Of course, it is our human nature to want to feel part of a group, an already established structure, and this is what people usually mean when they ask the question.

Although there is nothing like a baptism in Buddhism, there is a formula whereby one can commit oneself to the Buddhist training. This formula can be undertaken by one privately or at the feet of a Buddhist monk or teacher.
It is called taking refuge and what we take refuge in is the triple gem.

I have included this in its traditional way and language and once recited one can, with confidence, consider oneself as part of the global Buddhist community.
Of course, this is a serious commitment and should not be undertaken lightly.

A small ceremony to enhance the deeper feeling of spirituality can be performed using a Buddha statue, candles and incense.
Kneeling in front of this small shrine with hands in an attitude of prayer (anjali), one can recite the following:

BUDDHAM PUJEMI
I pay respect to the Buddha. (bow)
DHAMMAM PUJEMI
I pay respect to the Dhamma. (bow)
SANGHAM PUJEMI
I pay respect to the Sangha. (bow)

NAMO TASSA BHAGAVATO ARAHATO SAMMA
SAMBUDDHASSA
NAMO TASSA BHAGAVATO ARAHATO SAMMA
SAMBUDDHASSA
NAMO TASSA BHAGAVATO ARAHATO SAMMA
SAMBUDDHASSA
*Homage to the Blessed One, the Exalted One, the Fully
Enlightened One.*

BUDDHAM SARANAM GACCHAMI
I take the Buddha as my refuge.
DHAMMAM SARANAM GACCHAMI
I take the Dhamma as my refuge.
SANGHAM SARANAM GACCHAMI
I take the Sangha as my refuge.

DUTIYAM PI BUDHAM SARANAM GACCHAMI
(for the second time I take ...)
DUTIYAM PI DHAMMAM SARANAM GACCHAMI
(for the second time I take...)
DUTIYAM PI DHAMMAM SARANAM GACCHAMI
(for the second time I take ...)
TATIYAM PI BUDHAM SARANAM GACCHAMI
(for the third time I take...)
TATIYAM PI DHAMMAM SARANAM GACCHAMI
(for the third time I take ...)

TATIYAM PI SANGHAM SARANAM GACCHAMI
(for the third time I take ...)
The Five Precepts:

PANATIPATA VERAMANI
SIKKHAPADAM SAMADIYAMI
I undertake the rule of training to refrain from harming any living beings.

ADINNADANA VERAMANI
SIKKHAPADAM SAMADIYAMI
I undertake the rule of training to refrain from taking anything, which has not been freely given.

KAMESU MICCHACARA VERAMANI
SIKKHAPADAM SAMADIYAMI
I undertake the rule of training to refrain from misusing the senses.

MUSAVADA VERAMANI
SIKKHAPADAM SAMADIYAMI
I undertake the rule of training to refrain from wrong speech.

SURA-MERAYA-MAJJAPAMADATTHANA
VERAMANI SIKKHAPADAM SAMADIYAMI
I undertake the rule of training to refrain from taking drinks or drugs that tend to cloud the mind.

By reciting this formula and bowing three more times, you are now a Buddhist.

Walking the Path

Glossary of terms

Alms round:
The monks practice of collecting food once a day. Never begging.
Anapanasati:
Mindfulness of Breathing.
Anicca:
The law of impermanence.
Anatta:
The teaching of 'no abiding self'.
Arahat:
Someone enlightened by following the teachings of a Buddha.
Bhikkhu:
Buddhist monk. (nun: bhikkhuni)
Buddha:
A self enlightened being. The historical Buddha of our age is Siddhartha Gotama.
Buddhism:
Practice of the teachings of the Buddha.
Dukkha:
The inherent unsatisfactory-ness of life.
Metta Bhavana:
Loving Kindness.
Patimokkha:
The two hundred and twenty seven training rules of the monk.
Satipatthana:
Traditional name for Insight meditation.

Sangha:
Traditionally community of Arahats but now more generally,
all Buddhists.
Vipassana Bhavana:
Insight Meditation.

Acknowledgements

No book ever writes itself, and although the idea always seems simple, the actual work of sharing ones thoughts in a coherent way demands the help of others.
In this respect I feel blessed to have been aided by the people listed below, for their help, support and expertise.

Sayadaw Rewata Dhamma, my late teacher and the first person to read this work and approve it.
Isabelle Kewley, my wife, supporter and friend, who typeset the words and made them into the book you are holding.
Frank and Sheila Vaughan, who kindly proof read the second draught of the book without any prompting from me and who have helped in many ways.
Katja Rewerts, friend, supporter and disciple of Dhamma, who as always offered her services to promote Dhamma by volunteering once again to give this book, as with other books of mine, her invaluable assistance and its final proof reading.

To these people I humbly offer my gratitude. Without them how would I be?

It is said that when the disciple is ready the master appears, perhaps also we can say that when the master is ready, the disciple appears.

Once again I thank you for your presence in my already blessed life.

Walking the Path

About the author

Michael Kewley is the former Buddhist monk, Paññadipa, and now an internationally acclaimed Master of Dhamma, presenting courses and meditation retreats throughout the world.
A disciple of the late Sayadaw Rewata Dhamma, he teaches solely on the instruction of his own Master, to share the Dhamma, in the spirit of the Buddha, so that all beings might benefit.

Full biography of Michael Kewley can be found at:
www.puredhamma.org

Also by Michael Kewley

HIGHER THAN HAPPINESS
OPENING THE SPIRITUAL HEART
NOT THIS
LIFE CHANGING MAGIC
THE OTHER SHORE
LIFE IS NOT PERSONAL
THE REALITY OF KAMMA

Lightning Source UK Ltd.
Milton Keynes UK
13 December 2010

164312UK00001B/32/A